10 things
knowing about
THE NEW
TESTAMENT

G000153323

PHILIP
GREENSLADE
CWR

© CWR 2017

Published 2017 by CWR, Waverley Abbey House, Waverley Lane, Farnham, Surrey GU9 8EP, UK. CWR is a Registered Charity – Number 294387 and a Limited Company registered in England – Registration Number 1990308.

The right of Philip Greenslade to his own writings has been asserted by him in accordance with the Copyright, Designs and Patents Act 1988, sections 77 and 78.

The views and opinions expressed in this book are solely those of the author and do not necessarily represent those of the Publisher

See back of book for list of National Distributors.

Design and production by CWR.

Cover image: yuelanliu

Printed in the UK by Page Bros, Norwich.

ISBN: 978-1-78259-750-6

Acknowledgements

I dedicate this book to all those 'ordinary' Christians who love the Bible and want to understand it better. Especially I have in mind my friend, Roger Ball, who came on several of my courses and liked to talk theology. Roger went to be with the Lord earlier this year, and so this is written in his memory.

I would also like to pay tribute to my friend Greg Haslam on his retirement as Pastor of Westminster Chapel, to thank him for his own commitment to biblical teaching and for his consistent encouragement of mine over many years.

Thanks also to the enthusiastic 'Bible Discoverers' at Waverley, whose friendship and hunger for the Word for God is a constant motivation. Again I owe a debt of love to my wife, Mary, who did so much to make this book happen..

Contents

Introduction

Jesus never wrote a book. He left it to others to do it for Him.

With the full facts of Easter and Pentecost available to them, they would be in a position to explain and enlarge the message of Jesus. They bear witness to Him in preaching and teaching *and writing*, and it is His voice we hear speaking through them. What is subsequently written in Epistles and Gospels is essentially His testimony; the New Testament is essentially His book.

Luke's two-part work of the Gospel of Luke and the Acts of the Apostles makes the link. In the first verse of Acts, Luke says that his first book was about what Jesus had *begun* to do and teach, implying that his second book will be about what Jesus *continues* to do and to teach.

The Holy Spirit is the key to this, as Jesus promised:

'But when the Helper comes, whom I will send to you from the Father, the Spirit of truth, who proceeds from the Father, he will bear witness about me. And you also will bear witness, because you have been with me from the beginning.' (John 15:26–27)

The writers of the Gospels and the letters had to be selective in what they recorded:

'This is the disciple who is bearing witness about these things, and who has written these things, and we know that his testimony is true. Now there are also many other

things that Jesus did. Were every one of them to be written,
I suppose that the world itself could not contain the books
that would be written.' (John 21:24–25)

Even those who were not with Him from the beginning can claim
access by the Spirit to the 'mind of Christ' (1 Cor. 2:16). Through
them, the ascended Lord can explain Himself, and interpret
His work more fully and with pastoral application to the needs
and challenges of the churches birthed by the gospel. So, the
apostolic letters have been described as the posthumous epistles
of the ascended Christ. Jesus speaks through them (2 Cor. 13:3).

John's Revelation is first given to the glorified Jesus to show,
by way of an angelic messenger, to His servant John. John, in
turn, is told to: 'Write what you see in a book and send it to the
seven churches' (Rev. 1:1–2; 1:11).

There is much that has never been told. But what we *do* have
written for us in the New Testament is enough – more than
enough – to bring us to faith and eternal life.

As with the Old Testament Scriptures, so with the New. Without
some grasp of the bigger picture, we tend to stick to our favourite
parables, such as that of the prodigal son, or passages like 1
Corinthians 13. But in order to understand the Bible, we need
to look at it holistically. This book, along with its companion title
Ten things worth knowing about The Old Testament, is a starter
kit to help you get re-acquainted with the Bible, and the story of
Jesus. Through it, I hope you will be able to set those precious
passages in context and to see them shine even brighter.

As you read the New Testament, may you be switched on to the gospel it heralds, and your mind be lit up with truth.

May your imagination be fired with visions of glory.

May your heart burn within you as the Scriptures are opened to you.

May you be convinced that nothing can separate you from the love of Christ.

And may the power of His saving life and love flow into you through His living and active Word.

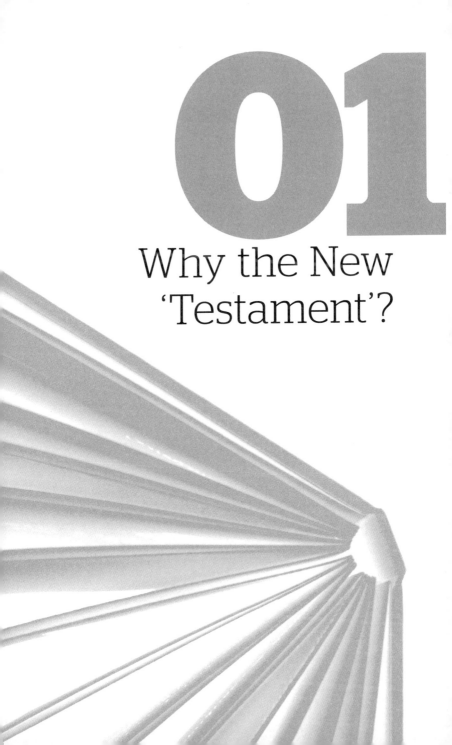

01

Why the New 'Testament'?

It is worth knowing why we call it the New 'Testament'.

From the moment Jesus said, 'This is the new covenant in my blood' (Luke 22:20), the writing of the New Testament became inevitable.

The English word 'testament' is a translation of the Greek word 'covenant'; but why 'inevitable'?

It arises from two considerations:

1. What is a covenant without a death?
2. What is a covenant without a document?

See how the two are connected when the first covenant was established with Israel through Moses:

> '[Then Moses] took the Book of the Covenant and read it in the hearing of the people. And they said, "All that the LORD has spoken we will do, and we will be obedient." And Moses took the blood and threw it on the people and said, "Behold the blood of the covenant that the LORD has made with you in accordance with all these words."' (Exod. 24:7–8)

Notice how the blood of the covenant and the book of the covenant together make good the covenant relationship between God and His people.

A new covenant

So why a *new* covenant? It was not that the old one wasn't good, but that the people had failed to abide by it and so find life in it.

The prophets Jeremiah and Ezekiel promised this new covenant. And what was promised through Jeremiah was a new way of making the covenant work, based on the thoroughgoing and lasting forgiveness of sins, and the writing of the covenant law on the very hearts of God's people. Such is its significance that Jeremiah's announcement (31:31–34), when reproduced in Hebrews 8:6–13, is the longest quotation from the Old Testament to be found in the New Testament.

Add to this Ezekiel's emphasis on the dynamic role played by the Holy Spirit in creating new hearts and new spirits, which are attuned to pleasing and obeying God from the 'inside out' (Ezek. 36:25–27). This new covenant experience bids fair to be a description of the Christian life as brought about by the apostolic preaching of the gospel (see Acts 2:22–42). So those who proclaim this gospel, and pastorally implement it, are 'ministers of the new covenant', operating as agents of the life-giving, transforming power of the Spirit (as in 2 Cor. 3:4–6). Everything now is predicated on the basis of the Easter achievement of Jesus.

At Sinai, the people had responded to the old covenant by effectively saying: 'All that the Lord has spoken, *we will do*.' The new covenant rests on the more secure foundation of Jesus saying to the Father: 'Not my will but Yours be done'; in effect, 'All that you have spoken *I will do* – and do for the sake of sinners.'

The new covenant relationship, inaugurated by Jesus, is both sealed with His blood and spelled out in His book.

Given the covenantal nature and function of the Old Testament Scriptures as a whole, it would be natural to those looking to experience the reality of the new covenant to expect written documents to emerge, sooner rather than later, that testified to the new covenant, explained it, and implemented it. It is no coincidence that the overall structure of the Old Testament has left its stamp on how the New Testament itself is structured.

A covenant treaty, as we have seen, implies a covenant text. In the ancient world, covenant text followed a basic formula:

> 1. Name the king whose subjects the people had become (Exod. 20:1; Deut. 4:35).
> 2. Summarise the history of their relationship (Exod. 20:1; Deut.1:1–4:49).
> 3. State the basic rules that govern the relationship ('the ten words'; Exod. 20:2–17; Deut. 5:1–33).
> 4. Spell out how these basic rules cover all aspects of life (Exod. 21; Leviticus; Deut. 12–16); with the sanctions for violating the agreement ('blessing/curses'; Deut. 27–28).

Naming the king, summarising the relationship

The New Testament, our new covenant document, works in a broadly similar way. By analogy, we have four Gospels placed first (though written later than most of the letters), which focus on who Jesus is, and on His saving mission that takes Him to the cross. These Gospels constitute the foundational covenant charter for Christians, grounding our identity in the storyline of Jesus, His authoritative words (which fulfil the law), His sacrificial death (which seals the new covenant) and His representative resurrection (which vindicates Jesus and His people, and inaugurates God's new creation).

Rules of engagement

The covenant text would then spell out the terms of the relationship, its responsibilities and obligations made – as in the Torah. Similarly, in the Sermon on the Mount, Jesus intensifies the law ('unless your righteousness exceeds that of the Pharisees…') and speaks as Himself being the source of its authority ('But I say unto you…') in keeping with the in-breaking of the kingdom of God through Him. It is possible that Matthew is consciously mirroring the first five books of the old covenant (the Pentateuch) by arranging his Gospel around five-major blocks of Jesus' teaching, each marked by the phrase 'when Jesus had finished' (His teaching or parables).

Effectively, the New Testament apostles correspond to the Old Testament prophets, whose one basic objective was to refute erroneous teaching and living and recall both kings and people to loyalty to the covenant. And isn't this broadly what we have in the apostolic letters? The apostolic writers exhort and encourage the new believers in Christ to understand the glory of being in the new covenant, urging them to cultivate the fruits of the Spirit.

Intriguingly, the promise of blessing and the warning of curse, so characteristic of the Old Covenant, bookends the book of Revelation (Rev. 1:3; 22:18–19) and might equally frame the whole of the New Testament construed as a new covenant document.

An expected Testament

The writing of the New Testament was to be expected in a second important sense. It was truth whose time had come:

> 'Long ago, at many times and in many ways, God spoke to our fathers by the prophets, but in these last days he has spoken to us by his Son, whom he appointed the heir of all things, through whom also he created the world.'
> (Heb. 1:1–2)

Here the 'long-ago' revelation of God, which was true but partial, is contrasted with the full and final revelation that has come through Jesus, of whom those earlier scriptures were in every sense prophetic. As Charles Hill argues, this makes the emergence of the New Testament inevitable:

'The authorisation and eventual existence of a New Testament canon is implicit in and guaranteed by the very act of redemption accomplished by Jesus.*

Commissioned as 'ministers of the new covenant', what did the apostles and evangelists and their trusted associates and scribes do? They began to write!

Finally, the newness of the New Testament as the new covenant document depends on the gift of the Holy Spirit. Jesus never wrote a book. He gave the Holy Spirit to others so that they would write it for Him:

'These things I have spoken to you while I am still with you. But the Helper, the Holy Spirit, whom the Father will send in my name, he will teach you all things and bring to your remembrance all that I have said to you.'
(John 14:25–26)

Jesus did not fully explain Himself prior to the cross – nor could He. The disciples struggled to comprehend His passion predictions ahead of time:

'His disciples did not understand these things at first, but when Jesus was glorified, then they remembered that these things had been written about him and had been done to him.' (John 12:16)

It's as if John is saying: 'Now we've got it straight.' Now the Gospel itself is stamped with the authority of the Holy Spirit.

Jesus did not fully explain the truth because He Himself *was* the great fact of truth to be expounded. He did not glorify Himself; He left the Holy Spirit to do that (John 16:12–15). What was initially puzzling to the first hearers of the good news would be made gloriously plain to them by the Spirit after the cross and in the light of the resurrection. The enigmatic Jesus of Nazareth becomes the eloquent Christ proclaimed in Philippi, and Colossae, and Rome or wherever – and eulogised in writing in letters sent to His new followers in those places.

Although Jesus never wrote a book, we may truthfully say that, by the Spirit, the New Testament we have in our hands is His book, in every respect His legacy, and His new covenant testament.

*Charles Hill, 'God's Speech in these Last Days' in Lane Tipton and Jeffrey Waddington (Eds.), *Resurrection and Eschatology* (Phillipsburg, NJ, USA: P&R, 2008), pp203–254.

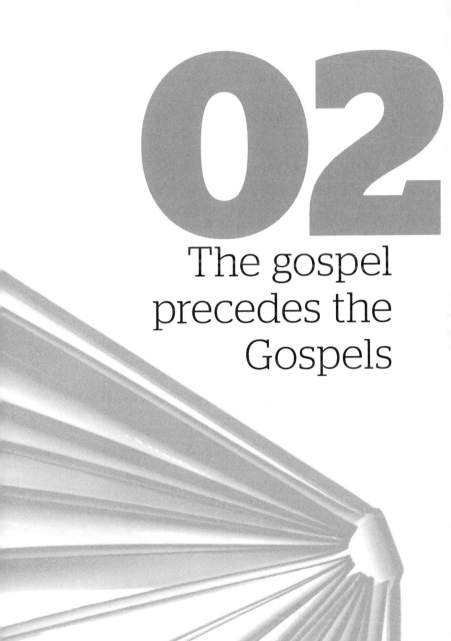

02

The gospel precedes the Gospels

It is worth knowing that the preaching of the gospel preceded the writing of the Gospels.

In the beginning was the gospel.

Our starting point is 1 Corinthians 15:1–11 – one of the earliest pieces of evidence for what the first Christians thought and believed:

> 'Now I would remind you, brothers, of the gospel I
> preached to you, which you received, in which you stand,
> and by which you are being saved, if you hold fast to the
> word I preached to you— unless you believed in vain.'
> (1 Cor. 15:1–2)

To begin with, it is important to note that the concept of 'gospel' or 'good news' derives from two main sources.

Firstly, we learn from the prophet Isaiah that 'good news' is not a blank cheque to be filled in as we desire. 'Gospel' in Isaiah comes with a clearly defined content – the good news to the exiles that God is returning to the centre of His people's life again, to reign over them, bringing forgiveness, peace and freedom. 'Gospel', therefore, is something God *does* (see Isa. 40:9; 52:7; 61:1–4).

Secondly, in apostolic times, the word 'gospel' also had political connotations. It was a propaganda term used in Roman official edicts celebrating something like the emperor's birthday or a recent military victory. At a time when an emperor cult that heralded Caesar as 'Lord' and 'Saviour' was emerging, a 'gospel' proclaiming Jesus in such terms would potentially be a very provocative, counter-cultural statement. One couldn't relativise Roman rule without consequences.

Good news!

For the apostles, the gospel is a message about what God has done *in* Jesus, what God has done *to* Jesus and *for* Jesus – which is why it is good news for us:

> *'because if you confess with your mouth that Jesus is Lord and believe in your heart that God raised him from the dead, you will be saved.'* (Rom. 10:9)

The gospel declaration about Jesus matches the earliest Jerusalem preaching of Peter, which climaxes:

> *'Let all the house of Israel therefore know for certain that God has made him both Lord and Christ, this Jesus whom you crucified.'* (Acts 2:36)

This is a startling announcement: that the recently crucified carpenter from Nazareth is now God's exalted right-hand Man, to be recognised as King of Israel (Messiah) and Lord of the world!

The message of the gospel is both proclamation – what God has done to Jesus, and promise – salvation for all who believe. Peter presses home the saving implication:

> *'And Peter said to them, "Repent and be baptised every one of you in the name of Jesus Christ for the forgiveness of your sins, and you will receive the gift of the Holy Spirit."'* (Acts 2:38)

For his part, Paul insists to the Corinthians that nothing in his gospel preaching or their experience is more important than this compressed summary of the Jesus story:

> 'For I delivered to you as of first importance what I also received: that Christ died for our sins in accordance with the Scriptures, that he was buried, that he was raised on the third day in accordance with the Scriptures, and that he appeared to Cephas, then to the twelve.' (1 Cor. 15:3–5)

Let's briefly reflect on the essentials.

1. 'Christ died' – a fact. And He died by crucifixion; a more brutal and degrading death could scarcely be imagined. It was reserved by the Romans for runaway slaves and political rebels. But the bare fact of his death is only good news as an *interpreted* fact – that Jesus Christ died *for our sins* 'according to the Scriptures'. Here the Old Testament helps us give meaning to His death by showing how animal sacrifices substituted for sinners (Leviticus), and by paving the way for the prophetic promise of a unique suffering-servant of God, who by His self-offering would transcend the old system by taking the 'iniquities of us all' upon Himself (Isa. 53).

2. 'He was buried' – at once a stark reminder of the harsh fact of death, and a sign of the glorious physical reality of His resurrection, underpinned by the empty tomb tradition of the Gospels.

3. 'He was raised on the third day in accordance with the Scriptures'. The bodily resurrection of Jesus is an act of God ('was raised'), which no one witnessed. That Jesus is bodily alive again beyond death is attested by any number of human witnesses, some of whom are 'still alive' as if Paul is implying, 'You can check this out with them!'

Jesus' bodily resurrection out of physical death and burial is crucially important because it is God's startling vindication of who Jesus is and what He achieved by dying for us:

'And if Christ has not been raised, then our preaching is in vain and your faith is in vain... For if the dead are not raised, not even Christ has been raised. And if Christ has not been raised, your faith is futile and you are still in your sins.' (1 Cor. 15:14,16–17)

Believing in the bodily resurrection of Jesus is indispensable to faith. In accordance with the Scriptures, Jesus was raised from the dead 'in accordance with the Scriptures'. A proof-text for resurrection in the Old Testament is hard to find – perhaps Hosea 6:1–3. But more likely, here is an echo of Ezekiel's great vision of the restoration of Israel conceived of as a resurrection from the dead (Ezek. 37). What might be hoped for on a national scale or at the end of time happens to Jesus, solo and in the middle of history, to show that He is one who embodies Israel's destiny and enacts God's strategic plan of salvation for the world.

Note how 'according to the Scriptures' undergirds Peter's preaching of the gospel in Acts 2, citing Joel and the Psalms. To say 'in accordance with the Scriptures' is to paint a big picture. The New Testament writers drew on great swaths of the Old Testament, tracing the contours of the new covenant gospel in the patterns and prophecies and storylines of the Old. And it was Jesus who first made these connections:

'And he said to them, "O foolish ones, and slow of heart to believe all that the prophets have spoken! Was it not necessary that the Christ should suffer these things and enter into his glory?" And beginning with Moses and all the Prophets, he interpreted to them in all the Scriptures the things concerning himself... Then he said to them,

*"These are my words that I spoke to you while I was still
with you, that everything written about me in the Law of
Moses and the Prophets and the Psalms must be fulfilled."
Then he opened their minds to understand the Scriptures'*
(Luke 24:25–27,44–45)

'According to the scriptures', then, is Paul's way of saying that
without the Old Testament, we cannot begin to understand
Jesus. Paul always has in view the larger narrative thought
world in which he has been trained – the story of Israel in the
Old Testament and her vocation to be the light to the nations.

After his conversion on the road to Damascus, Paul did not
discard the Old Testament Scriptures. Nor did he convert
from Judaism to another 'religion' – Christianity. What he had
seen no doubt left him in great anguish that he'd been wrong
about Jesus. Jesus was not the discredited messianic pretender
whose followers deserved to be stamped out, but the one now
vindicated and glorified after His cruel death and installed as
Israel's true Messiah and the world's true Lord.

Paul found himself with the Spirit-inspired task of
reconfiguring his beloved Old Testament, rearranging his
deeply held Jewish convictions in the bright new light of
the risen Jesus. What emerged was the Christ-centred, God-
energised, biblically integrated gospel that converted the
Corinthians when Paul first preached it to them.

The Corinthians, as we do, owe everything to this
gospel:
· They heard this gospel preached to them.
· They believed it was genuine and received it with
  faith.
· They 'stand' in this gospel as the sound basis of
  their lives.

> · They are being saved by it. They hold fast to it,
> knowing their lives depend upon it. It is the only
> sure foundation.
> Like us, the Corinthians, needed to be 'reminded'
> (v1) of what the gospel really is. The gospel needs
> to be remembered. It gives access to the fountain
> of life; it is the gift that goes on giving.

Apostles

Finally, notice 1 Corinthians 15:11: 'Whether then it was I or they, so we preach and so you believed.'

This is a very important statement. Paul recognised that he had been given a privileged post-ascension revelation, as if out of proper sequence (1 Cor. 15:8) and he values this first-hand experience. But at the same time, Paul never thought that his gospel message was unique to him. Three years after his encounter on the Damascus road, Paul went up to Jerusalem and spent 15 days with Peter. We can safely assume they didn't spend their time talking about the weather – but about Jesus, and agreed on their shared understanding of the gospel.

Even the Judean Christians – naturally suspicious of Paul's reported change of heart about Jesus – were reassured by the fact that 'He who used to persecute us is now preaching the faith he once tried to destroy' (Gal.1:23).

Notice the telling phrase 'the faith'. Paul is preaching the same message as the earliest Judean Church; not any faith but *the* faith – indicating an already settled body of truth. The modern allegation that Paul complicated and corrupted the original simple message of Jesus is totally wrong – Peter and James would surely have noticed and corrected him if he had. Nor does the apostle James, as is sometimes suggested, contradict Paul when he says that 'faith apart from works is dead' (James 2:26). Paul would have agreed. Paul is talking about how we enter into salvation, James about the outcome – how new life issues in good works. When Paul visited Jerusalem 14 years later, he met the big three – Peter, James and John – and they endorsed his ministry. Any tension that arose between the Jewish matrix of the faith and the far-flung Gentile reach of the gospel was answered by Word and Spirit at the great Synod in Jerusalem under James' leadership (Acts 15), from which emerged some tactical wisdom (on which all agreed).

Didn't Paul and Peter fall out? Yes, they did, once. But not over the gospel itself; only how it was being lived out. Paul accused Peter not of having a different gospel, but of not practising what he was preaching. Each apostle or New Testament writer has a distinctive voice and addresses a different situation. But variety does not mean contradiction. There is diversity, but within an overall unity of message and spirit. The apostles were, as we say, singing from the same hymn sheet.

Notice that Paul reminds the Corinthians that what he received he 'passed on' to be 'received' in turn by them. This is the semi-technical language of 'tradition', the transmission of truth in the oral cultures of the ancient world (which is why this fragment of text in Corinthians is so fascinating a glimpse of what the earliest Christians believed).

The time-scale here is only 18–20 years since Jesus had died and risen. Trace the sequence backwards:

Paul is writing around AD 55. He preached at Corinth around AD 50–52.

He received by revelation in the desert and from the others apostles around AD 33–34.

Christ has personally appeared to him around AD 32.

In other words, we are back to within two to three years of the crucifixion. The rapid expansion of the Church owed everything to the Spirit and the potency of the message, which worked in every place and culture. It was to nurture and guide a speedily growing Church that the apostles wrote, addressing problems and arguing theology with passionate pastoral urgency.

It is these letters we will consider next.

The rapid expansion of the Church owed everything to the Spirit and the potency of the message, which worked in every place and culture.

03

Letters first

It is worth knowing that many of the apostolic letters were written *before* the Gospels, and are the earliest written evidence we have of what the first Christians believed.

We don't normally read other people's mail – except when it comes to the apostolic letters in the New Testament!

Letter-writing was highly prized in the ancient world. By the standards of the time, most of the New Testament letters are unusually long and would have taken time and effort to produce. Let's take Paul as an example, and imagine how it may have worked.

Writing an apostolic letter

Paul has called another team meeting – for the third day running. It's in the morning because the light is better. The group hears a progress report on the letter Paul urgently feels needs to be sent to the church in question.

A secretary sympathetic to the message has been hired, whose language skills were up to the task; someone as competent as Tertius (Rom. 16:22), one hopes. Materials have been purchased, new or second-hand, wax tablets perhaps or sheets of parchment, cut to size, lined, then folded and stitched into codex-like notebooks.

Did the cost of production ever become an issue? Parchment could be washed and re-used, but even so, a letter as long as Romans might set them back some £1,500 in today's money.

No wonder Paul was always thankful for the generosity of the churches, like the Philippians – Philippians 4:15.

The secretary works slowly. Writing with a reed pen and ink on rough parchment calls for care and patience. The idea that such letters were dashed off in a hurry is mistaken. It is estimated that the letter to the Romans might have taken up at least ten hours of a proficient secretary's time.

No slapdash dictation or shorthand will have been used here. The secretary painstakingly takes down what is being said as Paul speaks freely and fiercely but also welcomes input from Timothy and Silvanus (1 Thess. 1:1). By all accounts, it was a distinctively Christian thing to mention one's associates in this way and suggests that they contributed to the contents of the letter.

On this particular morning, the team are ready for the draft letter to be read back to them. Under Paul's supervision, any final additions and amendments are made until Paul can assume apostolic responsibility for the letter.

Paul sometimes adds a postscript and signs off the letter in his own handwriting: 'I Paul, write this greeting with my own hand. This is the sign of genuineness in every letter of mine; it is the way I write' (2 Thess. 3:17). And to the Galatians he seems to acknowledge the poor light or ironically his own poor eyesight: 'See with what large letters I am writing to you with my own hand' (Gal. 6:11).

It remains only to entrust the letter to a reliable courier – someone like Tychicus (Eph. 6:21; Col. 4:7–8) – and the vital apostolic message is on its way.

What happens at the receiving end?

From the crowded tenement buildings of downtown Imperial Rome or its port of Ostia, or from the rougher areas around the harbour at Corinth, the poorer Christians would gather in the atrium of a wealthier Christian's house. The host, leader or presiding elder of the church would read the letter aloud as if Paul himself were standing there speaking to them (2 Cor. 10:9–11). It's unlikely that any such letter would be read just once only to be stashed away in a cupboard; surely it would have been brought out again and again to be expounded bit by bit (as the roots of expository preaching).

Reading the letters

Reading 'other people's mail' in the New Testament is like listening to one end of a telephone conversation. Most New Testament letters were written to address a specific situation, and the more you can understand that original situation and why the letter was written, the better you can appreciate it today's world.

Paul does write to individuals, like Philemon, Timothy and Titus. But for the most part, like the other apostolic letter writers, Paul is speaking to the church – in Corinth or Rome, or wherever. (There are few singular sheep in the New Testament: nearly all the 'yous' are plural!)

It's important to remember that the letters were not written *to* us, but they were certainly written *for* us. Let's look very briefly at some of those letters now.

1 Corinthians

In his first letter to the Corinthians, Paul responds to news of serious divisions in the church he had planted. Intriguingly, Paul mentions a previous letter he had sent now lost (1 Cor. 5:9). Since then, other contentious issues have been brought to his attention which he needs to address as a matter of pastoral urgency (1 Cor. 5:1; 7:1; 8:1).

The major cause of the trouble in the church surrounds the

way they are misusing the gifts of the Spirit. Paul rejoices in their spiritual giftedness but urges them not to get 'puffed up' with pride over what are undeserved gifts of God's grace (1 Cor. 1:4–8; 4:6–7). With great irony, Paul mocks the presumption that they have spiritually 'arrived', citing the paradoxical lives lived by him and his fellow 'fools for Christ's sake' (1 Cor. 4:8–13). This is as counter-cultural as it gets, but it's what the cross commits us to.

Paul strongly opposes any kind of boastful 'super-spirituality', because there is no authentic ministry of the Holy Spirit that bypasses the cross. Paul never backs away from the charismatic gifts, but he gives careful teaching on how they might be exercised. Similar confusion over the nature of the resurrection inspires a passionate response. Only if Christ is bodily raised from the dead are we Christians at all and is our work for God not in vain (1 Cor. 15).

2 Corinthians

2 Corinthians features Paul's sustained defence of his own ministry, which the Corinthians have downgraded because of Paul's track-record of suffering and trials. Rather than disqualifying him as not 'spiritual enough', such a chequered history bears all the hallmarks (and scars) of an authentic servant of the crucified Jesus. Notice, too, how passionate Paul is about gathering money to be sent to the hard-pressed Jerusalem church (2 Cor. 8–9). The cross calls us today to self-giving at every level.

Galatians

In his most combative letter, Paul rebukes those who are pressing Gentile converts to submit to the full panoply of the Jewish law (in particular, to be circumcised). Paul fiercely resists this idea as undermining the gospel of grace and Christian freedom. Faith is the only entry requirement – and

Paul finds biblical support for this in the story of Abraham (Gal. 3:1–29: 4:1–7). Our salvation and Christian freedom still depends on this truth.

Philippians

The letter to the Philippians can claim to be the most famous 'thank you' note in history Paul joyfully recognises the partnership between himself and the church, and uses this letter as an opportunity to urge his friends in Philippi to stand firm and united in the face of social pressures as living models of the self-giving mind-set of Jesus (Phil. 2:1–11). We are to have this mind-set among ourselves.

1 and 2 Thessalonians

Paul writes to the Thessalonians because they have been unsettled by a rumour that the 'day of the Lord' has already come in some secret rapture no one had noticed! Where did that leave them? Behind? And what of Christians who had already died? What was their fate? Paul writes to correct false teaching and to comfort troubled hearts (1 Thess. 4:13–5:11). In a subsequent letter he warns against an end-times teaching that breeds pride, complacency and idleness (see 2 Thess. 3:6–15). Clear teaching is needed now, as then, on the true nature of our Christian hope.

James

Context is everything when it comes to the letter of James. When James writes, he has been the leader of the church in Jerusalem since Pentecost, and writes as an authorised apostle of 'the Lord Jesus Christ, the Lord of glory' – quite an epithet to apply to your brother!

And he has a word for the hour. Palestine in the AD 50s was a volatile powder-keg. The social tensions that had swirled around Jesus had intensified. The air was thick angry voices and competing claims. The metropolitan elite, the lordly Sadducees, were still playing their self-interested power games with the Roman authorities, keen to protect their landed estates. Disenfranchised peasants were being stirred to revolt by vocal rabble-rousers. The extremist Zealots were hotly advocating armed rebellion. The Roman occupiers threatened violence to quell the angry dissent. And in the middle of it all were the small Christian communities whom James oversaw.

What pastoral advice could James offer in such a situation? James knew that careless talk costs lives. Inflammatory speeches could be the spark to ignite a forest fire (James 3:5–6). He wanted Christians to play no part in this incendiary war of words. Religious fanaticism, then as now, is not a mark of Christlikeness.

Drawing on the Old Testament's wisdom tradition in Proverbs and citing the example of Job, James assumes the great truth-claims of the gospel and cuts to the chase: 'Wise up; think before you speak. Keep your voices down. Lower the heat of the rhetoric. Let your actions speak louder than words.'

This is no therapy session aimed at comfortable believers wanting to hone their speech patterns.

James is writing an urgent 'tract for the times' – his times, and ours:

'By his own wish, the Father made us His own sons
through the Word of truth that we might be, so to speak,
the first specimens of his new creation.'
(James 1:18, J.B. Phillips)

We live in a post-truth world confused by fake news. But Christians are created by 'the word of truth', which is the gospel.

In the end, the world is changed not by those who shout loudest, but by those who listen hardest. This is 'wisdom from above' (James 3:13–18), the wisdom of the peaceable and gentle followers of Jesus who might just turn out to be 'the first specimens' of a new kind of people in a new kind of world.

1 and 2 Peter

The apostle Peter wrote two letters preserved for us in the New Testament. How stirring they are, reflecting Peter's own intense personal experience of Jesus. Peter's first letter opens: 'Peter, an apostle of Jesus Christ.' What a story that tells! Behind a conventional letter opening lies a stirring history of grace. He writes as a 'witness of the sufferings of Christ' (1 Pet. 5:1), who had earlier been among the 'eye-witnesses of his majesty' on the Mount of Transfiguration (2 Pet. 1:16–18). Let us look briefly at the letters of Peter, the 'rock' on whose confession of Christ the Church was built (Matt. 16:17–18).

Peter's first letter is addressed to the 'exiles of the dispersion', probably in a two-fold sense. His readers are 'in exile' geographically, scattered throughout Asia Minor. At the same time, they are 'exiles' metaphorically – citizens of another kingdom, feeling increasingly marginalised and threatened by the dominant pagan society all around them as do many Christians today.

Writing from the heart of that Empire (1 Pet. 5:13), Peter urges them to withstand the intense pressure of an honour-shame culture by not being ashamed of the cruciform way of Jesus, and by joyfully suffering the social stigma of belonging to Him.

Israel's vocation to 'be holy as I am holy' is now applied by Peter to Christians, not so that they might rebel against Rome, but so that they might dare to be as different as God is different. True 'sojourners and exiles', Peter assures them have been freed by the blood of Jesus from futile inherited ways of doing things to be just this kind of distinctive people (1 Pet. 2:11–12).

In saying all this, notice how Peter is indebted to the Old Testament Scriptures – spot the references to the law, the Psalms and the Prophets.

Above all, Christians are those who have been born again to a living hope through the living and lasting word of the gospel, and are destined to enjoy an imperishable inheritance (1 Pet. 1:3–4). This hoped-for inheritance though 'kept in heaven' is not that we go to heaven when we die (true as that may be), is not just for life after death but for a life beyond life-after death. It is a new earthly hope for which we will need new resurrection bodies. Only in his second letter does Peter give us a glimpse of this new world coming – 'the promised new heavens and the promised new earth, all landscaped with righteousness' (2 Pet. 3:13, *The Message*).

1 and 2 Timothy and Titus

Paul's most intimate and personal letters were those sent to Titus, a close associate, and Timothy, whom Paul has fathered as his 'son' in the faith (1 Tim. 1:2). These three letters preserve Paul's famous last words (1 Tim. 4:6–8), and also mark a crucial transition in which Paul hands on the apostolic gospel to Timothy and Titus as the next generation, committing them to 'guard the deposit' entrusted to them, as he himself had done (2 Tim. 1:13; Titus 1:3).

Another fragment from Paul's second letter to Timothy especially worthy of our consideration is this:

> '*When you come, bring the cloak that I left with Carpus at Troas, also the books, and above all the parchments.*'
> (2 Tim. 4:13)

The 'cloak' is understandable because winter was coming on (2 Tim. 4:21). But what of the 'books' and the 'parchments'?

The 'books' Paul wanted brought to him were probably OId Testament scrolls. But what are the parchments that 'above all' matter most to Paul? In all likelihood, they were copies in notebook form of all the letters Paul had written to the churches (a common practice at the time).

Keeping copies

When Paul's letters eventually came to be part of the canon of Scripture, it was probably not as a result of someone going round the Mediterranean world soliciting the letters from all the different churches. It is much more likely that Paul himself already had a collection of copies of his letters.

Perhaps Luke inherited this priceless collection and looked after it in Rome after Paul's death. Even the 'lost' letters may not be the fault of a careless church losing them, but of Paul not choosing to copy them. Certainly when Peter is in Rome – from where he writes his second letter – he is in the only place where he would have seen this collection. Peter confirms this in a wonderfully quirky human note:

> 'Our good brother Paul, who was given much wisdom in these matters, refers to this in all his letters, and has written you essentially the same thing. Some things Paul writes are difficult to understand. Irresponsible people who don't know what they are talking about twist them every which way. They do it to the rest of the Scriptures, too, destroying themselves as they do it.'
> (2 Peter 3:14–16, *The Message*)

Let's be aware of three things here: that Peter has access to 'all' of Paul's letters; that he acknowledges that Paul is sometimes difficult to understand and can be interpreted irresponsibly; and thirdly – and perhaps most significantly – that Peter clearly ranks Paul's writings with the other Scriptures.

The eventual inclusion of Paul's letters in the authorised canon of the New Testament was not an innovation of the third-century Church under political pressure, but was merely the official endorsement of a Scriptural authority that had begun to be recognised from the very earliest days of the Church. And it began with the apostle Peter praising the apostle Paul. How wonderful!

When reading the Apostolic Letters, always pay attention to the context.

04

Four angles
of vision

It is worth knowing that the four Gospels are four angles of vision on the same gospel.

Each of the four Gospel writers begins to tell the story of Jesus by linking Him to the previous stages of God's story told in the Old Testament Scriptures. Each Gospel opens by showing that what has gone before is crucial to understanding who Jesus is and why He has come.

And the starting-point is pushed further and further back. A simple graph makes this obvious:

$$\begin{array}{rl}
\text{Isaiah/Exile} < \ < \ < & \text{Mark} \\
\text{Abraham} < \ < \ < \ < \ < & \text{Matthew} \\
\text{Adam} < \ < \ < \ < \ < \ < & \text{Luke} \\
\text{God/Eternal Word} < \ < \ < \ < \ < \ < \ < \ < & \text{John}
\end{array}$$

Mark says that to understand the significance of Jesus, we must go back at least to the Babylonian exile in the sixth century BC, and the prophetic hopes raised then by Isaiah (see Isa. 40). God's people will be comforted and forgiven, and brought home to the Promised Land, with God returning with them to rule at the centre of their life again.

A voice in the wilderness prepares the way of the Lord for this – and Mark associates this with the ministry and message of John the Baptist, the forerunner for Jesus. Matthew accepts this account, but suggests that to understand Jesus we have to go further back in history – to David, and even as far back as Abraham and God's promises to bless all nations though him the note on which Matthew's Gospel ends. Luke, in effect, says that to understand Jesus, we must trace His story right back to Adam. The genealogy of Jesus as presented in Luke 3:23–38 shows the impact of Jesus on the whole human race – for Jew and Gentile – which anticipates the account in Acts of how the message about Jesus spreads out into the whole world. For his part, John agrees with all that the other Gospel writers have said, but pushes the roots of the Jesus story even further back into the eternal nature of God Himself and the creation of the world (John 1:1–5).

So we have four evangelists writing four Gospels, each with their own angle of vision, not contradicting but complementing one another. All four agree in presenting the story of Jesus not as an fairy-tale freak show of strange goings-on, nor as a bolt-from-the-blue invasion of divine power into human history, but as the conclusion of a much longer story – the story of Israel, which in turn (as John highlights) is the focal point of the one creator God's plan for His world.

Mark's Gospel

Mark is a great book – not least because it was, as far as we know, the first Christian book about Jesus to be written and circulated. So much of Mark's content is reproduced in Matthew and Luke that most contemporary scholars view Mark as the original Gospel.

In AD 64, a great fire lasting two weeks ravaged Rome. Conspiracy theorists suggested that Nero had started the fire to clear space in the city for his grandiose building projects. Stung by the insinuation, the Emperor sought to suppress the rumour by fabricating scapegoats – and Christians were an easy target, many being crucified in the arena or torn apart by wild beasts. So the church in Rome was a suffering church.

Mark's Gospel was written to fortify faith in tough times, and he did it by recounting the story of their suffering Saviour and Lord. Mark was with Peter in Rome around this time (1 Pet. 5:13) and it is perfectly feasible that Mark includes Peter's story and reflects the first-hand authenticity and authority of a chosen apostle of Jesus.

We may structure Mark's Gospel like this: eight chapters to say who Jesus is (Mark 1:1–8:30), and eight chapters to say that He is going to die (Mark 8:31–16:20).

Who is Jesus?

Jesus is presented as the fulfilment of Isaiah's hoped for end-of-exile (Isa. 40), which featured a voice in the wilderness (now identified as John the Baptist) preparing the way for the coming of the Lord (now identified with Jesus), and bringing about a new and greater exodus than the first one from Egypt or the later homecoming from Babylonian exile. The final 'rescue' from slavery to sin – and alienation from God – is now underway through God's royal Son, Jesus (1:9–11).

Mark presents Jesus as proclaiming the gospel of the kingdom of God – God's saving rule – breaking into human life through His words and healing miracles as a foretaste of a God's future kingdom. But, as the parable of the sower establishes, the kingdom comes like a seed sown into the ground whose working is mysterious (Mark 4:26–29).

Miracles and parables conceal as much as they reveal; they do not so much spell out the truth as draw people towards truth. Mark presents this as part of the 'secret' that is Jesus Himself:

'And he said to them, "To you has been given the secret of the kingdom of God, but for those outside everything is in parables"' (Mark 4:11).

The paradoxical nature of Jesus ministry provokes questions more that it gives answers and stirs up conflict and controversy – He commands silence and deflects testimony. Some scholars have called this 'the messianic secret' in Mark. What happens at Caesarea Philippi is a turning point:

> *'And he asked them, "But who do you say that I am?"*
> *Peter answered him, "You are the Christ." And he strictly*
> *charged them to tell no one about him.'* (Mark 8:29–30)

The secret is partly unveiled but still kept under wraps. The truth that Jesus is Israel's true King and Messiah is revealed to Peter; but what kind of Messiah will Jesus be? The second half of the Gospel addresses this for us.

Why does Jesus die?

In a famous over-statement, the Gospels have been called passion narratives with introductions. One third of Mark is devoted to the last week of Jesus' life, and the cross undoubtedly looms large over chapters 8–15. In three passion predictions, Jesus curiously refers to Himself in the third person as 'the Son of Man' (Mark 8:31; 9:31; 10:32). 'Son of Man' can simply mean 'mere mortal' (Ezek. 2:1), but the way Jesus employs the term alludes strongly to Daniel 7. There we read that one 'like a Son of Man', apparently having destroyed the beasts, comes in glory to the throne of the Ancient of Days to be vindicated, and to receive the kingdom and its authority – which He shares with 'all the saints of the most high' whom He incorporates (Dan. 7:13–14,21–22,27).

Jesus paradoxically fuses the ideas of suffering with the glory associated with the title 'Son of Man', so sustaining the air of ambiguity and mystery that surrounds Him. It is as if He is saying: 'Don't box me in to your preconceived ideas as to how a messiah should behave. Don't jump to premature conclusions about me. Watch this space. Await further developments – and, crucially, wait until my death and resurrection before you decide who I really am.'

So Jesus's anticipated 'coming in clouds with great power and glory' (Mark 13:26) more likely refers primarily not to His second coming, but to His vindication as Israel's human representative after suffering, and His exaltation to the right hand of God with all authority (see Mark 13:14–27; Matt. 28:18–20).

Mark 13 startlingly unveils the mystery: that the coming of the kingdom of God, long-awaited as the true climax to Israel's story, would entail not the exaltation of Jerusalem and the Temple but the destruction of both city and sanctuary. Israel's hope is re-defined in Mark's Gospel as going down into death with Jesus, her Messiah, in hope of being raised to a new life as the community of the Messiah, re-constituted as the people of God around Him.

Jesus' identity as 'the Son of God' is confirmed three times – said to Jesus (Mark 1:11), to the disciples (Mark 9:7), and declared at His crucifixion by a Roman centurion (Mark 15:39). Jesus warns us repeatedly that discipleship will be costly. But for the Roman Christians – perhaps already suffering for their faith – it was perhaps a sweet irony and huge encouragement to learn that it was a Roman centurion who had been the first to confess Jesus as the Son of God!

Jesus' secret is now well and truly out – and the resurrection confirms it and evokes a world-mission to bear witness to him, the risen one, as Israel's true king and the world's true Lord.

Let's stand back for a moment and reflect on what a 'gospel' is. What kind of literature is it?

In the nineteenth century, the Gospels were regarded simply as records of the life of Jesus. Clearly they are not like modern biographies – details are sparse as to His birth and childhood and the silent years until His adult maturity. Currently there is a new appreciation of the Gospels as a distinctive type of ancient biographical literature – containing highly selective material about a person, which is told for a particular theological, didactic, apologetic or pastoral purpose.

We read Mark as a vivid and fast-paced narrative that reads like a script for an action movie. His Greek is relatively unsophisticated, making it like the tabloid on the gospel news stand! Mark seems to have been the first to link the idea of 'gospel' (*euangellion*), first used in the public preaching of what God has accomplished in Jesus, to a written narrative of what Jesus had said and done.

Matthew and Luke appear to have used Mark's account as the basis for their own – furthermore, some 250 verses are common to Luke and Matthew but are not found in Mark. Matthew and Luke then add their own discrete sources to their individual Gospels.

So, why more than one Gospel? Well, partly because there was so much to tell!

'Now there are also many other things that Jesus did. Were every one of them to be written, I suppose that the world itself could not contain the books that would be written.'
(John 21:25)

In fact, Paul tells the Ephesian elders in Acts 20:35 to 'remember the words of the Lord Jesus, how he himself said, "It is more blessed to give than to receive"' – words of Jesus you won't find in any of the four Gospels!

The Gospel writers were not mere reporters but literary craftsmen, selecting and shaping their material in distinctive ways that add colour and richness to our picture of Jesus. They used oral testimonies, that is, the recollections of eye-witnesses and ear-witnesses to what Jesus had said and done (see Luke 1:1; John 21:24), and written testimonies – probably made on the wax-tablets then coming into common use for taking notes.

The Gospel of Matthew

Matthew starts his story of Jesus with a stylised genealogy divided into three blocks of 14, in order to show that the story of Jesus can be understood only in the light of the earlier stages of the story told in the Old Testament Scriptures.

Three markers are key:
- Abraham – in whom 'all nations will be blessed' (Gen. 12:1–3; Matt. 8:10–11; 28:18–20)
- David – the king as 'son of God' in whom the nation's destiny as 'God's son' is embodied (Exod. 4:2–23; 2 Sam. 7:14)
- The Babylonian Exile – the backdrop for understanding the mission of Jesus who has come to inaugurate the new and greater exodus by leading God's people out of death and into resurrection. He will do what only Israel's God can do. (Matt. 1:21–23)

From the beginning of his Gospel, Matthew repeatedly emphasises the theme of fulfilment, and the terminology is often in the mouth of Jesus Himself (Matt. 13:14; 15:7; 21:42). Notice the programmatic statement from the lips of Jesus:

'Do not think that I have come to abolish the Law or the Prophets; I have not come to abolish them but to fulfil them' (Matt. 5:17)

To 'fulfil' the prophets does not mean to tick off a list of prophetic proof texts that land on target in Jesus. Something much bigger is going on. Jesus completes and 'fills-full' all that the previous stages of the story promised to achieve.

How does Matthew see this working out?

As the new *Israel*, Jesus recapitulates Israel's story as her Messiah. He re-runs that story to bring it to its God-intended goal. This is symbolised by His coming up out of Egypt (2:13–15) and by His victory over temptation, succeeding as the 'son of God' where Israel and her kings had failed, citing Deuteronomy to refute the tempter's thrust: 'If you are the Son of God…' (Matt. 4:1–11).

As a new *Moses*, Jesus comes through water (by His baptism in the Jordan) into the Judean wilderness to a mountain where He delivers 'the Sermon on the Mount' – spelling out the royal law of God in its new covenant phase of administration and with unique authority ('But I say to you…').

As a new *Joshua* (Yeshua), Jesus will 'save' His people from their sins and lead a new conquest of 'enemy territory' – healing the sick, delivering from demons and summoning disciples, so spearheading the invasion of the saving rule and reign of God.

As the new *David*, Jesus is welcomed at street level as saviour (Matt. 21:9; 22:41–46) coming as a Davidic king to his city, his throne and his temple (Matt 21:1–17). But He is a different kind of Davidic king; riding on a donkey rather than a warhorse (Matt. 21:1–10; see Zech. 9:9); and rejected, not received, by the ruling authorities (Matt. 21:42–43).

But still the ultimate question hangs in the air: who are You? By what authority do You do and say these things (21:23), claiming to fulfil God's covenant law (Matt. 5:17) and re-assigning the leadership of the 12 tribes to men of Your choice (Matt. 10:1; 19:28)? A critical moment in all four Gospels is

Jesus's provocative piece of street theatre at the Temple, which threatens its very existence, provoking His arrest and death.

Matthew ends his story with Jesus – much like Moses in Deuteronomy – gathering the remnant of Israel (His own disciples) around Himself on a mountaintop. But unlike Moses, Jesus says in effect, 'Go, not just into a Promised Land but into the promised world. Teach people not what the Torah says, but what I have commanded you.' Even more remarkably, the pledge is not, 'Yahweh will go with you', but '*I* will be with you to the end of the age'! Here is Emmanuel – 'God with us' in person, at whose royal command a new covenant people is launched on the world with a restored Abrahamic mission to bring the blessings of God's salvation and grace to all the nations.

The Gospel of Luke

Luke introduces his gospel by assuring us of his credibility.

> *'Inasmuch as many have undertaken to compile a narrative of the things that have been accomplished among us, just as those who from the beginning were eyewitnesses and ministers of the word have delivered them to us, it seemed good to me also, having followed all things closely for some time past, to write an orderly account for you, most excellent Theophilus, that you may have certainty concerning the things you have been taught.'* (Luke 1:1–4)

Attempting to take further what his predecessors had done, Luke writes like a historian in the Greek tradition carefully scrutinising his sources and assuring Theophilus, his sponsor, of his integrity. It may be that Luke set out to continue the biblical history told by the Old Testament Chroniclers and was perhaps even conscious that he was writing Scripture.

Luke is convinced that the Jesus story is not something happening 'in a corner' (Acts 26:26) but impacts the whole of the Gentile world. So he sets it on a world stage, synchronising his account of the story with the wider events of world history going on at the time (see Luke 2:1–2; 3:1–2).

Matthew tells the world's best story as a very Jewish story; Luke tells a quintessentially Jewish story as the world's story. So Jesus is 'a light for revelation to the Gentiles and for glory to your people Israel' (Luke 2:32). The irony is acute. Little did Augustus Caesar realise that a large stone was being dropped in his political pond and that the ripples would reach Rome (as in the book of Acts, Luke's 'volume two').

In his infancy narratives, Luke is evoking the birthing of Israel's monarchy, re-working and paralleling the narratives of Davidic kingship in the nation of Israel. Mary's Magnificat (Luke 1:46–53) echoes the song of Hannah (1 Sam. 2:1–10). John the Baptist is playing, as it were, the part of Samuel to Jesus' David. Like Samuel with David before him, John the Baptist recognises Jesus as the true King. How different His servant-kingship will be, and how liberating His royal manifesto.

In the distinctive central section of his narrative (Luke 9:51–19:11), Luke's special emphasis is that Jesus is on a journey to Jerusalem. It is not a straight-forward travel itinerary: Jesus makes many detours on the way. It is a theological and spiritual journey, not the shortest distance between two points, but the direct route to doing His Father's will and facing the destiny that awaits Him.

Jesus appears to be sovereignly able to avoid premature death, though the leaders in the community and angry mobs try to bring this about (Luke 4:28–30). Luke describes the journey to death as His 'exodus' (Luke 9:31), leading to His being 'taken up' (Luke 9:51). Jesus' journey to Jerusalem is achieving a new Exodus; a redemptive path to the glory of the Father. Along the way, often in memorable parables unique to Luke (for example those of the Good Samaritan and the Prodigal Son,) Jesus challenges His disciples to follow Him on this costly journey down a road that leads to life.

In the last week of his life, before His crucifixion, the religious leaders demanded to know one important thing of Jesus: 'Tell us by what authority you do these things, or who it is that gave you this authority' (Luke 20:2). Only the cross and resurrection would begin to answer this. Jesus' death was as strange as His life. He died alongside political rebels and took the place of Barabbas, a revolutionary leader – although He Himself was not one. The Romans killed Jesus because they thought He was the Messiah, and so was a danger to them; the Jewish leaders rejected Him because they thought He wasn't the Messiah, and therefore dangerous to them!

He went to the cross – as Israel, for Israel. But the road will not end in Jerusalem. It will take Volume Two (Acts) to show how the story is taken on by those who belong to 'the Way' (Acts 9:2).

Significantly, Luke closes his gospel account with another journey – the journey of the two disciples on the road back to Emmaus. Luke describes the resurrected Jesus opening the eyes of the two disciples who reflected:

> *"Was not necessary that the Christ should suffer these things and then to enter his glory?" And beginning with Moses and all the Prophets, he interpreted to them in all the Scriptures the things concerning himself.'*
> (Luke 24:26–27)

No single passage in the New Testament can claim to be more important for unlocking the meaning of the whole Bible than this one. It is Jesus Himself who opens the Scriptures for us and opens our minds to understand them. All the previous stages of the story told in the Old Testament are gathered up and come good in Him. His life and death is shaped to the pattern of Exodus suffering and deliverance, and of Exilic 'death and resurrection'.

By His death, Jesus inaugurates the promised new covenant, releasing the blessings of Abraham to all humanity. By His resurrection He makes the first down-payment on a brand new creation – good news to be told to 'all nations' (Luke 24:47).

Timeline

4 BC	AD 27–30		AD 66–73
Birth of Jesus	Death and resurrection of Jesus		Jewish/ Roman War Fall of Jerusalem
		Galatians	Mark
		AD 49?	AD 64–65?

This last date, the destruction of Jerusalem and the Temple in the Roman-Jewish War around AD 70, is the most important event for understanding the background to Jesus and the New Testament and yet remains the best kept secret among readers of the New Testament!

All four Gospels present the story of Jesus as the conclusion of a much longer story.

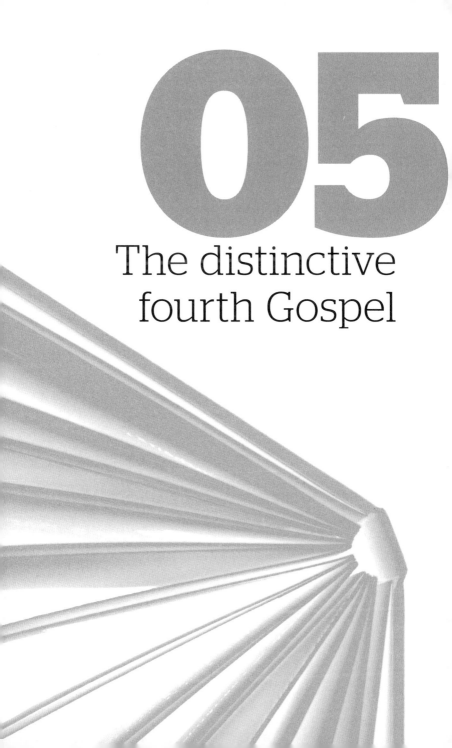

05

The distinctive fourth Gospel

It is worth knowing what makes the Fourth Gospel distinctive.

Even a cursory reading of the four Gospels alerts us to how distinctive John's Gospel is. John has no parables, no Sermon on the Mount, no Transfiguration, no Last Supper or Gethsemane. Instead, we hear Jesus delivering lengthy discourses and, seemingly going out of His way to draw attention to Himself.

These differences can be overdrawn; there is nothing in Gospel of John that cannot be shown to be there, at least in seed form, in the other three Gospels. Like the other Gospel writers, John is speaking about the same historical Jesus and is following the same outline of the story. In fact, it is to John's mention of three Passover feasts that we owe our view of Jesus' ministry as lasting three years and not one year.

The Word

The prologue of John 1 (vv1–18) contains all the seeds of subsequent development later in the Gospel. The creator acts to redeem His creation by the incarnation of the *Logos* or 'Word', who was in the beginning with God, and was God, and through whom all things were made (1:1–3).

By employing the word *Logos*, John maintains the crucial connection with the Old Testament. There God's 'word' inspires all creation (Gen. 1:1; Psa. 33:6) and brings revelation through the prophets (Isa. 55:10–11). By the author's time, 'Word' has the added significance of referring also to the preaching of the gospel message, the 'word' of Christ:

> 'And the Word became flesh and dwelt among us, and we have seen his glory, glory as of the only Son from the Father, full of grace and truth.' (John 1:14)

When Moses asked to see God's glory, he was answered by a revelation of God's name as merciful and gracious, full of steadfast love (Exod. 34:5-8), and it became Israel's confession of faith in her covenant Lord. Jesus is full of grace (steadfast love) and truth (faithfulness) because He is the full expression of God's character. He shows us God's glory. He manifests God's name (John 17:6).

For John, the whole of Jesus' life and ministry demonstrates the glory of God. This is perhaps why he omits to mention the transfiguration account as told in the other Gospels. In John, Jesus is not so much transfigured on one occasion but translucent all the way through His ministry. In his distinctive style, John fuses the glory Jesus later obtained with the humiliation He suffered on the cross. Being lifted up on the cross is, with hindsight, seen to be the true secret of His exaltation to glory (John 3:14; 8:28; 12:32).

Fulfilment

Even more than Matthew, John's is the Gospel of fulfilment. Jesus fulfils and replaces the significance and purpose of all of Israel's feasts and institutions, and so brings the whole scriptural narrative of the Old Testament to its intended goal and climax. It is in this comprehensive and conclusive way that all the Scriptures 'bear witness' to Jesus (John 5:39). This involves a radical break with Judaism and the inauguration of a whole new order of things – making John the Gospel of the new age, when the old wine is turned into the new wine.

Jesus presents Himself as a new Temple (John 2:13–21). The great Temple in Jerusalem, still under construction, was not only a centre of national identity but was God's 'earthly address', the place of God's concentrated holy presence on earth in the 'holy of holies', the centre of sacrifice that dispensed forgiveness. Whereas the other three Gospels place Jesus' radical action in the Temple in the last week of Jesus' life, John brings it forward to the start of Jesus' ministry as if all that Jesus did in the meantime was heading for this. Beyond Easter, the risen Lord Jesus is to be the dwelling place of God among men through whom forgiveness is dispensed.

- Jesus promises a new birth – a birth 'from above' created by the Holy Spirit, which will short-circuit inherited or ethnic privileges (John 3:1–15).
- Jesus offers fresh and living water and initiates a new way of worship in the Spirit of truth that satisfies the Father's desire for true worshippers (John 4:1–15).
- Jesus brings salvation as a new Sabbath day – not a day when God stops working and not so much a day of rest as a day of restoration, because Jesus does 'only what he sees the Father doing' and is working with him (John 5:1–20).
- Jesus provides by His death not the temporary manna given to Israel in the wilderness, but the new eternal bread from heaven (John 6:22–59).
- Jesus introduces a new Feast of Tabernacles. Where the original featured great lights and the pouring out of basins of water, Jesus declares Himself the source of living water and the giver of light to the world (7: 37–8:12).
- Jesus is the new and good shepherd, who lays down His life for the sheep (John 10:1–30).
- Jesus lays down a marker of the new creation by raising

Lazarus from the dead and speaking of Himself as 'the resurrection and the life' (John 11:17–44).

- Jesus gives a new commandment – an eleventh commandment that fulfils the other ten, and He promises a new era of the Holy Spirit to empower the new covenant community (John 13–16).
- Jesus is the New and great High Priest, whose consecration and continuing intercession protects His disciples and assures them they are loved with the same love with which the Father loves the Son (John 17).

Finally, John shows us Jesus newly enthroned as King – paradoxically on the cross (John 18–19) followed by His resurrection (20–21) on the 'eighth day of the week' – the dawn of a new creation.

John presents the death of Jesus as bringing the world to a point of crisis or 'judgment' for it and for its 'ruler' (12:31).

Jesus' whole life is a courtroom drama. Just as in Isaiah God is 'on trial' before the nations and calls Israel to bear witness to Him as the one true God, so now Jesus calls His disciples to bear witness to Him as the one who can truly say, as God does: 'I am' (See Isa. 43:8–12).

The real crisis is the challenge to faith. John speaks sparingly of the kingdom of God, choosing to emphasise the *present experience* of the kingdom of God in terms of having and enjoying eternal life now, through believing that Jesus is the Christ. For John, faith is both a believing 'that' – having certain convictions about Jesus as the Christ – and a believing 'in' – making a radical commitment to Jesus and enjoying an intimate relationship with Him:

> 'Now Jesus did many other signs in the presence of his
> disciples, which are not written in this book; but these are

written so that you may believe that Jesus is the Christ, the Son of God, and that by believing you may have life in his name.' (John 20:30–31)

Resurrection

This Gospel is distinctive for being the Gospel of the resurrection.

Only in the light of the resurrection can Jesus be properly understood. William Lane suggested that John was 'writing his Gospel from a vantage-point he did not himself enjoy during Jesus' earthly ministry'*. After Jesus' resurrection and ascension, the disciples were able to fully understand who He was and what He had achieved:

'When therefore he was raised from the dead, his disciples remembered that he had said this, and they believed the Scripture and the word that Jesus had spoken.'
(John 2:21–22)

It is a distinctive emphasis of John's Gospel that it is only with the hindsight of the Holy Spirit that Jesus is seen in His full glory. It is the Spirit who glorifies the Son and leads the disciples into the deeper and developing truth about Him (John 16:12–15). John's Gospel is an example of this very promise, and Gary Burge phrases it this way:

'For this reason, John's Gospel proves to be an empowering Gospel that shaped this Christian community so that it would expect dynamic spiritual experiences. Jesus and the Father were dwelling within these spiritually reborn believers. No other Gospel speaks like this.'**

All 'four' one, one for all

Finally, I want to draw attention to something important about all four Gospels. We call them the Gospels – plural – but strictly speaking, they are not. Rather, there is one gospel and four accounts of it as in the gospel according to Mark, according to Matthew, according to Luke and according to John.

The four Gospels, for all their fascinating variety, are four accounts of the *one gospel*.

The Gospels are *the* gospel – the saving story of Jesus. As in 1 Corinthians 15, the gospel is the public proclamation of Jesus, of what God has done to Jesus and for Jesus, and of what God has done in and through Jesus.

> 'Now Jesus did many other signs in the presence of the
> disciples, which are not written in this book; but these are
> written so that you may believe that Jesus is the Christ, the
> Son of God, and that by believing you may have life in his
> name.' (John 20:30–31)

All the evangelists speak with one voice on that.

**First and foremost, the gospel is the public
proclamation of Jesus.**

*William Lane, *Highlights of the Bible: Bible Commentary for the Layman*
(London: Regal Books, 1980), p41.
**Gary M. Burge, 'The Letters of John', *The NIV Application Commentary*
(Grand Rapids, MI, USA: Zondervan, 1996), p24.

06

Nothing can stop the gospel

It is worth knowing that nothing can stop the progress of the gospel!

The Acts of the Apostles is the second installment of a two-volume work composed by Luke, separated in the canon by the Gospel of John.

In Acts 1:1 Luke speaks of his 'first' or 'former' book, and it seems likely that the careful preface to his gospel (Luke 1:1-4) was intended to cover Acts as well. If so, then 'events fulfilled among us' most likely includes the stories told in Acts in which Luke himself participated; the 'among us' matching the famous 'we' passages (see Acts 16:10).

Like his Old Testament counterparts, the chroniclers, Luke writes prophetic history, narrating events as the actions of God. This sense of a divine agenda creating a divine momentum is carried on just as dramatically in Acts. According to Luke, events happen according to 'God's will' or 'counsel' (Acts 2:23; 4:28; 13:36; 20:27); in line with what 'is necessary' (Acts 3:21; 19:21; 23:11; 27:24); or as God 'foreordains' them (2:23; 4:28; 10:42; 17:31).

A gospel for all nations

Acts has a basic geographical structure showing the outworking of Jesus' prophetic vision:

'But you will receive power when the Holy Spirit has come upon you, and you will be my witnesses in Jerusalem and

in all Judea and Samaria, and to the end of the earth.'
(Acts 1:8)

Luke describes the apostolic witness moving from Jerusalem outwards through Judea and Samaria, reaching – symbolically at least – the 'ends of the earth' through the ministry of Paul in Rome (see Acts 13:17). Several major phases are marked by a 'Pentecostal' outpouring of the Spirit as if to endorse the move.

Luke's theological purpose underwrites the geographical adventures of Acts: firstly to show the continuity in the story, and to highlight the indissoluble link between Jesus and the Church.

And secondly, to emphasise the dynamic connection between the anointed Christ – 'Messiah' (meaning 'anointed one') and His Spirit-anointed community. The same Spirit who worked in and through Him is now available to and operative in His followers: 'And in Antioch the disciples were first called Christians' (Acts 11:26) – meaning 'the Christ-people'.

Luke's pastoral aim was firstly to vindicate the ways of God to his Gentile readership and give them a new sense of 'assurance', and secondly, to show that God's promises to Israel have not failed despite her rejection of his Messiah, and that the inclusion of Gentiles is in fulfilment of the Abrahamic covenant and God's intent to bless all nations. In this way Gentile believers are re-assured about the continuity of their position with God's age-old designs, and can be confident that their faith rests on a long and deeply-laid foundation.

Luke's apologetic purpose focuses on this vexed question of the relationship between national Israel and the Church, and the issue goes back to the Day of Pentecost.

Was Pentecost the 'birthday' of the Church, as is commonly supposed? Or was Pentecost the restoration of God's people, Israel, as the new covenant community, promised by the prophets?

Let's reflect on the fact that the first Christians did not simply cease to be Jews on the day of Pentecost. They continued to adhere to the Torah, and to attend the Temple. Secondly, the future of Israel had never been envisaged as a totally new beginning, but as the old Israel renewed and reconstituted – and it was on this basis (and as Jews to other Jews) that the apostles made their first appeal.

Thirdly, the fact the Jesus had so publicly and deliberately attached Himself to the revival movement of John the Baptist continued to be seen as a significant part of His story told in the early apostolic preaching (see Acts 1:5,22; 10:37; 13:24).

'Baptised by John' is as integral a part of His story as 'suffered under Pontius Pilate' – at least if we are to grasp the way in which Jesus brought the long story of Israel to its destined climax with an eye on the ends of the earth.

Chris Wright explains this new covenant community like this:

> 'Jesus was launched by a revival movement for the restoration of Israel. He launched a movement for the blessing of the nations. He himself therefore was the hinge, the vital link between the two great movements. He was the climax and fulfilment of the hope of Israel and the beginning of the hope of the nations.'*

In all likelihood, Old Testament anticipations of salvation would have led them to expect events to unfold in a particular sequence – Israel first, then the Gentiles! If the ingathering of the Gentiles was to occur, then Israel must first be restored. Hence their question to Jesus: 'Lord, will you at this time restore the kingdom to Israel?' (Acts 1:6)

What reversed the biblically expected sequence was the amazing and dramatic number of Gentiles who began to respond to the gospel while the Jewish synagogues resisted it. The conversion of Cornelius, and the success of Paul and Barnabas in Antioch and elsewhere, were the events that finally forced the hand of the apostles and elders at the great Jerusalem Council called to resolve the issue (Acts 15).

Under James' leadership, the Gentiles were 'officially' welcomed into the people of God. It was conceded that their incoming had to mean that, in some sense, the prophesied restoration of Israel under new Davidic kingship had occurred as the prophet Amos had indicated (Acts 15:13–21; Amos 9:11–12).

> The dramatic events described in Acts are best viewed not simplistically as the birth of the Church, but as the founding – from within Israel – of the new covenant community, which was always intended to include Gentile believers.

A church model for today?

Yes – and No!

No – if it means we think we can get back to a primitive, perfect Church. The 'Acts Church' has often been pressed into service by reformers in a radical pursuit of an original, 'ideal' church. But this is too idealistic. There never was a 'pure' Church that was only subsequently corrupted by tradition.

Take how the Church started. It was bad enough that Judas, chosen as one of the Twelve, had betrayed Jesus and then committed suicide, and before long, the apostles had to face the deception of Ananias and Sapphira (see Acts 5). We can never escape the scandal of belonging to the Church; it is for sinners, saved and being saved by grace, who are learning with others how to be truly human.

It is sometimes suggested that the church in Acts was an

interim until things settled down to a steadier, less spectacular pattern. Of course, we cannot turn back the clock to replicate the unique features of the original 'big bang' with which the Church's mission got started. But that does not mean we can consign the account to ancient history with little or no bearing on how we do church today.

Yes – because truth can be conveyed as powerfully through narrative (as in Acts) as it can through more propositional teaching (as in the apostolic letters). We should not preference the epistles over the Acts in quite so stark a way; surely we can assume that the apostles practised (in Acts) what they preached and taught (in the epistles).

Quality or quantity?

The Acts of the Apostles is bracingly realistic. It's helpful to consider the size and proliferation of the churches in that early period. By the end of the first century, it is estimated that out of a population of some 60 million in the Mediterranean world touched by the gospel, there were perhaps 10,000 Christians. There were no mega-churches then, either. Perhaps 100–120 believers gathered in each place, drawn from smaller house groups. This did not stop each church, however, being a sign and a foretaste of the kingdom of God.

Paul's prayers, which he refers to at the start of almost every one of his letters, never once contain a plea for more converts; only that those already converted might know God better. The emphasis appears to have been on making disciples – the standing orders of the church according to the 'Great Commission' (Matt. 28:19). His direction to baptise converts from every nation into the experienced reality of the life and love of the Trinity went hand in hand with training these disciples in the ways of Jesus Himself.

The Way

In Acts, Christians were first described as those 'belonging to the Way' (Acts 9; 19:23; 22:4; 24:14). Since 'the Way' is a way of suffering as well as a way of life, Christians are called to be Christ's witnesses even unto death (*martus* means 'witness'). We cannot be sure whether Luke consciously wants us to read martyrdom into his concept of witnessing, but it fits with his account of how the first Christians were called to replicate the cruciform style of Christ's own life by enduring opposition, legal trials, unjust suffering and possible death – all the while bearing witness to His resurrection. This is more than triumphalism – this is victory!

An unstoppable gospel

The first breakthrough in the advancement of the gospel came when the apostle Peter (arguably the main player in the first half of Acts) encountered the Gentile Cornelius. Cornelius' response to the gospel and reception of the gift of the Holy Spirit was a turning point in the way the gospel is recognised as effective beyond its Jewish matrix.

Paul (the major player in the second half of Acts) further replicated in his own preaching and ministry the story of Jesus as the fulfilment of Israel. Paul's priority, too, was to go *first* to the Jewish synagogues in the ancient world, and then to the Gentiles (see Acts 13:40–52; 26:16–18).

He too stood trial, as Jesus had done, for the 'hope' promised to the patriarchs of Israel (Acts 26:6). He made it his mission to show that God had been faithful in Jesus to His prophetic promises, and had brought Israel's destiny to a saving climax so that all who were 'appointed to eternal life' might believe (see Acts 13:16–49).

The big picture

In some ways we owe the very shape of our New Testament to Luke – in the ordering of the books, with Acts linking the Gospels and the epistles not just chronologically, but theologically. Just as Luke begins his Gospel with repeated emphases steeped in Old Testament prophecy on Israel's hope of redemption and restoration, so he ends his Gospel and begins Acts with the note of fulfilment of that hope flowing over into mission to the nations. As Jesus said, the gospel of the kingdom is like a mighty mustard seed, potent enough to expand from its obscure beginnings until its reach touches the whole earth.

Luke's gripping narrative inspires us to believe that the gospel leaps over all barriers. Nothing seems able to stop its progress; not national frontiers, not storms and shipwrecks, not evil opposition, not ethnic rivalries, not prison bars, not martyrdom – nothing stalls the momentum of the Spirit through the preaching of the gospel.

Significantly Luke's last word in the Greek text is 'unhindered'! Thankfully for us there were future chapters to be written. The story goes on!

In Acts we trace the saving journey of the gospel from Jerusalem to the ends of the earth.

*Chris Wright, *Knowing Jesus Through The Old Testament* (Basingstoke: Marshall Pickering, 1992), p166.

07

New humanity, new creation

It is worth knowing that the goal of the gospel is the creation by redemption of one new humanity, the pointer to a new creation.

Few other parts of Scripture have had such decisive influence at various stages in Christian history as Paul's Letter to the Romans. But Romans is not, as has been commonly supposed, a systematic doctrinal thesis, but rather a pastoral letter with one long argument.

Gordon Fee puts it like this:

> 'Romans is totally taken up with Paul's passion for the gospel whose goal is the creation by redemption of a single people for God's name both of Jew and Gentile.'*

The Romans 'symphony'

The assumption is often made that Romans simply tells us how to get saved. It is then viewed as if almost exclusively concerned with the doctrine of justification by faith. This truth does lie at the heart of Romans but it is set within a larger context and serves a larger purpose.

Paul makes an interconnected argument, like a symphony with four basic movements.

First movement: Romans 1–4
In Jesus, the Messiah, God has acted to show His covenant faithfulness by dealing with the sin of both Israel and the world

in the cross of his Son (Rom. 3:21–26). By this means, the one God creates a worldwide family of faith in line with His promises to Abraham, and His own deepest intentions.

(The question of ethnic Israel is put on hold until chapters 9–11.)

Second movement: Romans 5–8

This community of faith – created by the love of God in Christ and by the Holy Spirit – is the true fulfilment of Israel's vocation and forms the nucleus of a brand new humanity. This is the Spirit-empowered people through whom God announces and furthers His plans for the whole of creation.

Third movement: Romans 9–11

These three chapters reveal Paul's emotional turmoil over this issue he has postponed until now: Given Israel's almost total rejection of Messiah Jesus, do God's covenant commitments still stand? The cross is the means of resolving this problem and thus achieving the redemption of Israel and the salvation of the world. This opens up the astonishing paradox that the failure of Israel was somehow built into the plan from the beginning, thus highlighting the mystery of God's grace and sovereignty and vindicating His integrity. We may well appreciate how Paul, in contemplating this, is simply lost in wonder love and praise (Rom. 11:33–36).

Fourth movement: Romans 12–16

Having died and risen with Christ in baptism, empowered by the Holy Spirit to do what pleases God, the new community is called to live as the new humanity, living shrewdly with godly wisdom in a pagan society (Rom. 12:1–13:14) and united in heart, fellowship and mission.

Paul prays:

> 'that together you may with one voice glorify the God and
> Father of our Lord Jesus Christ. Therefore welcome one
> another as Christ has welcomed you, for the glory of God.'
> (Rom. 15:6–7)

Since no special Jewish privilege counts, Gentiles are welcome,
but must embrace a crucified Jewish Messiah. And since there
is no room for Gentile arrogance, Jews are welcome, but have
to reconnect with the Abrahamic roots of their story by sharing
their Messiah with all nations. It is grace – not race – that
counts. If Jews only understood this, they would see and
embrace Christ; if Gentiles could see this, they would joyfully
receive Jews!

Why did this letter need to be written?

In AD 49, the Roman Emperor Claudius issued an edict
banishing Jews from Rome, apparently because of disturbances
instigated by someone called Chrestus – universally taken
as a reference to Christ – and this may have occasioned the
writing of the letter. If Jewish Christians were among the Jews
expelled in AD 49, then the newly emerging church would
have been stripped of its first leaders. In their absence, Gentile
membership and leadership would have become predominant.
When Christian Jews returned as Claudius' edict lapsed,
tension might well have arisen between Jewish and Gentile
sections of the church.

The call to unity in church was urgent, and the basis for it in
the gospel needed to be spelled out afresh – especially as Paul
has his eye on more distant horizons.

> So Paul writes to commend his gospel to the
> church in Rome around AD 56–57 for two main
> reasons:
> - A pastoral aim – to encourage the unity of Jewish
>   and Gentile Christians in the church (Rom. 12–15).
> - A strategic aim – to enlist the support of the
>   Roman church for his projected mission westward
>   into Spain (Rom. 15:20–24,28–29).

To achieve both these aims, Paul commends his understanding of the 'gospel'. Paul is convinced that this life-transforming message can revolutionise the entire Roman world with the news that Jesus, not Caesar, is Lord. Paul sees his ministry as a priestly activity offering up Gentile converts as a sacrificial offering to God (15:16). Paul sees himself as making known the deep prophetic mystery of God's strategic purpose of salvation, bringing many to obedient faith (16:25–27). If the heartbeat of Paul's message is the saving righteousness of God, then this is the programmatic statement:

> 'For I am not ashamed of the gospel; for it is the power of
> God for salvation to everyone who believes, to the Jew first
> and also to the Greek. For in it the righteousness of God is
> revealed from faith for faith, as it is written: "The
> righteous shall live by faith."' (Rom. 1:16–17)

For Paul, the justification of sinners by grace through faith in the achievement of Jesus is the vindication of God's character as Holy love (I encourage you to re-read Romans 3:3–4; 3:23–26). The justification of sinners serves the justification of God. It is a saving means to a more glorious end.

In Michael Bird's words:

> 'Justification is the act whereby God creates a new people, with a new status, in a new covenant, as a foretaste of the new age.'***

Romans 15:7–9 therefore is a significant summary statement of the letter: 'For I tell you that Christ has become a servant of the circumcised on behalf of the truth of God in order that he might confirm the promises given to the patriarchs, and in order that the Gentiles might glorify God for his mercy.'

The dimensions of salvation

The range and scope of what Jesus accomplished by His death and resurrection is extraordinary:

> *'In him we have redemption through his blood, the forgiveness of our trespasses, according to the riches of his grace, which he lavished upon us, in all wisdom and insight making known to us the mystery of his will, according to his purpose, which he set forth in Christ as a plan for the fullness of time, to unite all things in him, things in heaven and things on earth.'* (Eph. 1:7–10)

These words are an excellent synopsis of Paul's letter to the Ephesians to which we now turn.

Ephesians

The letter to the Ephesians is unusual in not being a response to any particular problem in the church. It represents the cream of Paul's theology, a holistic vision of God's plan through Jesus

Christ to re-integrate everything in his fractured creation. Where are Christians in this grand, redemptive scheme of things? Paul's answer is: 'in Christ' – his favourite definition of what being a Christian means. It suggests being incorporated *into* Christ, so that what happens to Him happens to us (Eph. 2:4–10). By grace, through faith, we are placed into the radical new order of things brought about by Christ's achievement.

Knowing our 'spiritual location' is crucial. If we know *where* we are ('in Christ') we discover *who* we are – those who are blessed, chosen, called, loved, adopted, redeemed, forgiven and sealed by the Spirit. In chapters 1–3, Paul celebrates this Christian identity, then, in chapters 4–6, he unpacks Christian vocation.

It follows that if you know where you are and who you are, then you will know what you are here for.

Paul implies strongly that the kind of behaviour and lifestyle spelled out in chapters 4–6 flows organically out of those identified as being 'in Christ'. This practical outcome is captured by the word 'walk' – a metaphor for living the way God desires.

We live this way because that's who we are. If I am acting in Hamlet I do not do things and say things as if I were in King Lear. The drama I am participating in is the cruciform story of an exalted Jesus Christ. Each day I am called to dress for the part, to 'put on Christ' not as a false disguise but as an authentic sign of the 'new self' I really am in Him (Eph. 4:22–24). Ephesians 4–6, then, can be construed as the challenge to express our true identity and live out of this different story as part of a new humanity. We can achieve this in the face of opposition only in the strength that God supplies (Eph. 6:10–20).

Our Christian calling, then, is to share in and herald the unity that God intends for His whole creation. This restoration of the original cosmic harmony is prefigured by unity at every level.

At a national level it involves reconciliation between ethnic groups – Jew and Gentiles – made into one new humanity by Christ's death on the cross (Eph. 2:12–14). At the church level, this blood-bought unity is demonstrated in the love and forgiveness Christians show to one another (Eph. 4:3, 25,32). This Spirit-inspired unity is now to be worked out at the level of the family and household (Eph. 5:19–32). Imagine a series of expanding concentric circles – from peace at home to peace in the universe, with church as the training ground for one and the sign of the other.

The real actor in the drama is God, who is at work in all things. It is the Father who plans and sources it all, the Son who sacrificially enacts it, and the Spirit who reveals it and empowers us to live it and bear witness to it. And it all tends 'to the praise of God's glorious grace', whose work it is (Eph. 1:6,12,14; as well as 1:11; 2:8–10).

Colossians

The letter to the Colossians complements the letter to the Ephesians, and was perhaps also a circular letter sent to the new churches in the Lycus Valley, including the one at Laodicea (Col. 4:16). It might well be described as a world-view letter. A world-view is not a mere system of thought or comprehensive philosophy; rather, it is a perceptual framework, a way of seeing what is true of all of reality. As J.B. Phillips translates it, 'We are asking God that you may see things, as it were, from his point of view' (Col. 1:9). Everyone has a world-view, whether they realise it or not. We need God's view of the world in which Jesus is the centre-piece, as celebrated in the magnificent 'Christ hymn' (Col. 1:15–21). It is astonishing that these stunning words are applied to someone who only a generation before had been discredited and crucified. Other possible early Christian 'hymns' speak of Jesus in equally fulsome terms, and lyrical language is seen in Philippians 2:5–11, Hebrews 1:1–4 and 1 Timothy 3:16.

In God's plan for redemption, everything is meant to radiate out from Jesus, to transform individual, domestic and community life. Paul is aware that the Colossians need re-envisioning because they are facing false teachers – who are arguing that their faith in Christ is not sufficient and needs to be augmented with a strange concoction of Jewish legalism and mystical experience. But Paul insists that Jesus Christ is enough, from start to finish. Nothing needs to be added to Christ, for in Him 'are hidden all the treasures of wisdom and knowledge', and 'in him the whole fullness of deity dwells bodily' (Col. 2:3,9).

Jesus plus nothing equals everything.

World-views are intended not simply to give us a theoretical vision of life, but always a practical vision for why and how we can live life and live it to the full. For Christians, Jesus is the centre of a God-shaped vision of reality, and He is all we need to live truly human lives restored by grace to be worthy of God.

When we understand who we are, we will know what we're here for.

[*]Gordon Fee, *God's Empowering Presence: The Holy Spirit in the Letters of Paul* (Peabody, MA, USA: Hendrickson, 1994), p473.

[**]Michael F. Bird, *The Saving Righteousness of God: Studies on Paul, Justification and the New Perspective* (Eugene, OR, USA: Wipf & Stock, 2007), p4.

08

Jesus fulfils the Old Testament

It is worth knowing that we cannot understand Jesus apart from the Old Testament – and vice versa.

The letter to the Hebrews makes this plain.

The author describes what he has been attempting to do: 'I appeal to you, brothers, bear with my word of exhortation' (Heb. 13:22). This is a term describing a typical message delivered in a synagogue, when the congregation would expect to hear the word of the Lord through an exposition of the lectionary readings drawn from the law and the prophets, as Paul did in Antioch (Acts 13:15; compare with Jesus in Luke 4:16–21). In Hebrews, then, we are eavesdropping on typical first-century preaching.

So, the letter to the Hebrews is based on a sermon or series of biblically based sermons re-affirming that the story of Jesus is the climax of the earlier part of the story, which concerned God's dealings with Israel. In fact, Hebrews is the most sustained exposition of the superiority of Jesus in the whole New Testament. Jesus is 'better' than angels, Moses, Joshua, Aaron – and so introduces a 'better' priesthood, sacrifice, covenant, and hope.

Ablaze with the glory of Christ, the message, at the same time, issues sombre warnings and offers strong encouragement. It speaks compellingly to a group of Christians tempted by a hostile society to blunt the cutting edge of its commitment to the uniqueness of Jesus Christ.

The tried-and-tested, flesh-and-blood humanity of Jesus offered on the cross qualifies Him for His ongoing post-ascension ministry as High Priest, and this magnificent truth strengthens the faith of those who are being tested:

'Therefore he had to be made like his brothers in every respect, so that he might become a merciful and faithful high priest in the service of God, to make propitiation for the sins of the people. For because he himself has suffered when tempted, he is able to help those who are being tempted.' (Heb. 2:17–18)

Keeping the faith

Hebrews is a pastoral message, sent as a letter to address the traumas of Christians in Rome during or after the Neronian persecution. With their faith coming under intense pressure, they would have been in need of strong reassurance – and Hebrews provides just this by facing them up to the cost of discipleship and concluding that it is a cost well worth paying.

The recipients of the letter were Jewish Christians who, under pressure in an 'honour-shame' culture, were in danger of reneging on their commitment to Christ and returning to Judaism.

The writer challenges them: Would they be so ashamed of Jesus or would they, like Moses, prefer the 'reproach of Christ' to the approval of society? (See Heb. 11:25–26; 13:13.) To encourage his readers to stand firm in their faith, the writer skilfully blends exposition and exhortation. The expository sections do not stand on their own, but provide the foundation for the exhortations.

Exposition followed by exhortation:		
1:1–14	followed by	2:1–4
2:5–3:6	followed by	3:7–19
4;1–5:11	followed by	5:12–6:12
7:1–10:18	followed by	10:19–39
11:1–12:13	followed by	12:14–29
Followed by the final words of		13:1–25.

Throughout his appeal, the preacher makes use of Old Testament categories, especially drawn from books such as Exodus and Leviticus – generally not the best read Old Testament books among contemporary Christians! This has led to the neglect of Hebrews in much popular Christian study and preaching. But Hebrews richly rewards careful study. We can be intimidated at first by all its talk of priests, sanctuaries and sacrificial ritual and we may ask: What does all this religious language have to do with reality? In one sense, nothing at all!

Jesus is the only priest, altar, and sacrifice we need for a lasting relationship with God. And yet, apart from Israel's story and scriptures and God-given worship, we would lack this rich and final vision of who Jesus is and what He has achieved.

No other book in the New Testament shows more clearly the interconnectedness of the two Testaments. Hebrews affirms our repeated mantra: Without the Old Testament, we cannot understand Jesus. Without Jesus, the Old Testament is incomplete. At the same time, no New Testament writer is more emphatic that Jesus is the climactic chapter in God's story:

> 'Long ago, at many times and in many ways, God spoke to our fathers by the prophets, but in these last days he has spoken to us by his Son, whom he appointed the heir of all things, through whom also he created the world. He is the radiance of the glory of God and the exact imprint of his nature, and he upholds the universe by the word of his power. After making purification for sins, he sat down at the right hand of the Majesty on high, having become as much superior to angels as the name he has inherited is more excellent than theirs.' (Heb. 1:1–4)

God spoke truthfully in the past. But what He spoke was *provisional* and *partial* – a prophetic heralding of the full revelation of God given in His Son. Jesus is the final word; therefore we are already in the 'last days'.

Hebrews takes us beyond the four Gospels, picking up the fully human story of Jesus where they leave off by tracing His human career post-ascension to His exaltation in glory, His being seated at God's right hand, His high-priestly ministry of continuing intercession, and His eternal Lordship in the 'power of an indestructible life' (Heb. 7:16).

Bringing it all together

After the raft of scriptural citations in chapter one, Hebrews revolves primarily around an exposition of seven key Old Testament passages, illuminating Christ and our life in Him.

Psalm 8:4–6 in Hebrews 2:5–18

The saving story of Jesus, the truly human one, redeems our Adamic humanness and with it the reason for Israel's covenantal existence. Jesus will bring 'many sons to glory', restoring the destiny from which we have fallen.

Psalm 95:7–11 in Hebrews 3:7–4:13

Hebrews draws out the typological parallels between the wilderness journey of the children of Israel towards the 'rest' of the Promised Land, and the pilgrimage of the Church towards the 'rest' of God's future. This concurs with the end of the letter, where our author speaks of the 'lasting city' for which Abraham left Ur at the start of the faith journey – the heavenly Jerusalem to which, in spiritual worship, we have already come.

Notice that the writer, in quoting Psalm 95, lets Scripture speak in the present tense. 'Therefore, as the Holy Spirit says, "Today, if you hear his voice…"' (Heb. 3:7).

Psalm 110 in Hebrews 5:5–7:28

Hebrews traces the redemption of the Adamic story through Abraham (and one greater than Melchizedek), to Moses (and beyond Sinai), through Joshua (and beyond the 'rest' found in the Promised Land,) until it is entrusted to 'great David's greater Son' (Heb. 1:5; 2 Sam. 7:14) – finally coming home to Mount Zion and to the sacrificial priest-king who rules there (Heb. 12:22).

Jeremiah 31:31–34 in Hebrews 8:6–10:18

At this point in the letter occurs the sharpest contrast with the previous dispensation and its institutions.

The references to Jeremiah's 'new covenant' in Hebrews 8:6 and 10:18 form bookends – so that everything said between these two quotations explains why the old covenant needed to be renewed. This quotation from Jeremiah 31:31–34 is the longest Old Testament citation in the New Testament. It is fundamental in describing the profound transformation brought about by the incarnation, atoning death, resurrection and glorification of Jesus and the gift of the Holy Spirit.

For all who believe, Jesus' sacrifice for sins is final and complete; His resurrection makes Him the permanent priest, and His ascension is His re-entry to the heavenly temple of which the earthly tabernacle was a mere replica:

> 'Therefore he is the mediator of a new covenant, so that those who are called may receive the promised eternal inheritance, since a death has occurred that redeems them from the transgressions committed under the first covenant.' (Heb. 9:15)

The new covenant has been inaugurated, and its promises have begun to be put into effect in the lives and experiences of all who confess faith in Jesus Christ. Who would want to retreat to the twilight shadows when the full light of a God's new day has dawned in Jesus Christ?

Habakkuk 2:3–4 in Hebrews 10:32–12:3

In the faith and faithfulness of the prophet Habakkuk, the author of Hebrews sees a model that stimulates him to make an extended challenge to his readers to live likewise. Once again, we are reminded of the simple truth that the 'righteous one shall live by faith'.

Proverbs 3:11–12 in Hebrews 12:4–13

The wisdom of Proverbs 3 serves as a catalyst for the Preacher who is eager to help sustain his beleaguered readers' faith as they live counter-culturally as disciplined but much-loved sons and daughters of God.

Exodus 19 in Hebrews 12:18–29

While there is no there is no direct citation from Exodus 19, the passage is clearly in the writer's mind as he pens Hebrews 12. He reflects on the smoking mountain of the Sinai narrative, which he connects with the eschatological shaking of the cosmos spoken of in Haggai 2:6 – to remind us that we have an 'unshakeable kingdom'.

Heroes of the faith

Finally, Hebrews offers us a roll-call of heroes and heroines of faith – but not so that we may choose our favourite role-model (not even Abraham or Moses or Gideon or Rahab are that!). Rather, the writer wants us to realise that these well-known figures are incomplete without us – and that we are all incomplete without Jesus!

The long faith story climaxes in Jesus and sweeps on to include us. We find ourselves drawn into the drama of God's redemptive purposes for the whole earth, called to participate in the out-working of His saving plan. We take up the baton of the Old Testament believers. We follow Jesus, never taking our eyes off Him on whom our faith depends from start to finish.

Hebrews represents expository preaching at its best – letting Scripture itself speak in the present tense.

09

'Apocalypse now'

It is worth knowing that John's Revelation contains nothing new – and is about worship!

'I do not read the Revelation to get additional
revelation about the life of faith in Christ... The truth
of the gospel is already complete, revealed in Jesus
Christ. There is nothing new to say on the subject. But
there is a new way to say to say it. I read the
Revelation not to get more information but to revive
my imagination.'* (Eugene Peterson)

Peterson's verdict grabs our attention, and if he is right (which
I believe he is), he raises the questions we need to ask right
from the start: What do you see? What do you hear? What do
you read?

John's Revelation defines itself in three ways: as an *apocalypse*,
asking us what we see; as a *prophecy*, asking us what we hear
and how we respond; and as a *message* sent in letter form, asking
us to hear what the Spirit is saying to us (Rev. 1:1–5).

Firstly, the book of Revelation defines itself as an *apocalypse*
from the Greek term *apocalypsis*, translated here as 'revelation'.
What Jesus gives to John is a dazzling vision that fires the
imagination. This accounts for the highly pictorial language
which, as we shall consider later, characterises the whole book.

*'The revelation of Jesus Christ, which God gave him to
show to his servants the things that must soon take place.
He made it known by sending his angel to his servant*

John, who bore witness to the word of God and to the
testimony of Jesus Christ, even to all that he saw.'
(Rev. 1:1–2)

Today, the word 'apocalypse' may conjure up Hollywood blockbusters or sci-fi end-of-the-world movies. But in John's time, a more ancient category of literature would spring to mind. Revelation displays the features of a classic genre in the ancient world, familiar to Jewish writers, called apocalyptic literature (of which the prophet Daniel is a prime example).

What does 'apocalyptic' literature do?

Apocalypse pulls back the curtain of 'normal' perception to show us two aspects of reality:

1. It take us 'behind the scenes' of our familiar world to show us what is going on right now in the transcendent realm of ultimate truth and authority even as we go about our everyday lives.

2. It shows us a glimpse of God's future, of where the story is going, what is the God-intended goal of all things.

In other words, John's apocalypse looks both ways. It looks up to God's throne, and from that vantage point looks down on the way things are, and it also looks forward to God's future, and from there it looks back on the present and to what things might become. It sets our 'here and now' in the light of God's 'there and then', and urges us to take heart from what we see.

Note the crucial chain of communication – from God to Jesus to an angelic messenger, and then to John and to God's servants (Rev. 1:1). One thing is clear: this revelation belongs to Jesus, is from Jesus, and is about Jesus. John receives this revelation as the 'word of God' and as the 'testimony of Jesus'; that is, the testimony Jesus himself bore to the truth about God as God's 'faithful witness' (Rev. 1:2,5).

But this word and testimony is a showing as much as a telling

– as the opening sentence indicates – implying that that book is meant to help us see what we would not otherwise see. What God achieves through Jesus is the resolution of our flawed history and the renewal of His creation. John is shown this in the downfall of the ungodly man-made city (represented by Babylon in chapter 18), and the down-coming of God's final holy city, the new Jerusalem of a new heaven and earth, in which God dwells with His people forever (Rev. 21–22).

Pictorial and symbolic

If there is then one thing worth knowing about John's Revelation – and apocalyptic literature in general) – it is this: the language and the numbers are *pictorial and symbolic*. The visual impact of the book's vivid symbols and dramatic images breach the mental and spiritual defences of its readers with mind-expanding imagination.

Understanding this might have spared the Church from many unhelpful interpretations of the book.

In keeping with the apocalyptic genre of writing, Revelation addresses real historical situations and speaks of real historical events, both in time and at the end of time but it does so in highly figurative language and images. If we try to interpret these images literally, we end up with utter fantasy and nonsense. What John depicts are the *symbols*, and not the reality the symbols represent. For example, Jesus is given all power and authority, but when we see Him, He won't look like a seven-horned, seven-eyed, sheep!

Similarly, virtually all the numbers in Revelation are symbolic. John employs wonderfully artistic patterns of fours, sevens, and twelves: four to speak of universality (every tribe, tongue, people and nation – used seven times! – and four winds or four corners of the earth); seven to speak of completeness (seven spirits, seals, trumpets, bowls, Beatitudes). Twelve is the number of God's people, squared for completeness and multiplied by 1,000 to indicate vastness (indeed, John sees a vast multitude too numerous to count – Rev. 7:4).

There is a skilfully crafted sequence to John's narrative of visions, but if we try to understand all this in strict linear chronology we end up in total confusion. For example, chapters 6–16 unveil a seven-fold pattern of judgments that are in parallel to one another. The order in which the visions are presented throughout the book does not depict what *happens* next, but what John *sees* next. So the visions are kaleidoscopic rather than chronological.

Interweaving threads

Secondly, the book of Revelation is a powerful *prophecy* that calls for obedience and faith and asks us 'what do you hear'?

Blessed is the one who reads aloud the words of this prophecy, and blessed are those who hear, and who keep what is written in it, for the time is near (Rev. 1:3).

Revelation is the only full-scale example of Christian prophecy in the New Testament. When John says he was 'in the Spirit', he is claiming to be in receipt of prophetic inspiration (1:10; 22:7,10,19, 20).

In Revelation, John stands indebted to the long line of previous prophets (Rev. 10:7; 16:6; 22:6,9). It is fascinating to note that Revelation has no direct or complete quotation from the Old Testament Scriptures. Yet the book is soaked in echoes and allusions to the Old Testament – not least from the prophets Ezekiel and Daniel. In this sense there is essentially nothing new taught in Revelation, but John superbly gathers up all the previous threads of biblical prophecy and weaves them into a great gospel tapestry. John sees the coming together of

Old and New Testament revelation.

The anthem he hears being sung by the victorious people of God is the 'song of Moses and the Lamb' (Rev. 15:3). Inscribed on the 'twelve gates' of the New Jerusalem are the names of the 12 tribes of Israel, and on its 'twelve foundations' the names of the 12 apostles (Rev. 21:9–14).

It is a significant point in this regard to note that what John hears is often interpreted for him by what he sees.

He hears that God's people number 144,000 (Rev. 7:4–8) and so is assured that God's people are complete with no one in who should not be there and no one out who should be in. But when he turns to look, he sees not merely 144,000 but a vast multitude too numerous to count (Rev. 7:9)!

Similarly, when John hears of a lion and turns to look, he sees a Lamb (Rev. 5:5–6). And the hearing and the seeing together assure us of the kind of victory God wins in Jesus; it is the triumph of sacrificial love, a triumph implemented by the followers of the Lamb who overcome by laying down their lives for His sake (Rev. 12:10–11).

Revelation is in this way a 'prophetic apocalypse' that gives a transcendent perspective on John's world. This world – enclosed by Roman power and propaganda – is broken open and put into the perspective of a larger, ultimate reality. The 'here and now' of the world as it is looks different from the vantage point of the 'there' (heaven/God's throne) and the 'then' (the final state of affairs).

John, of course, as a Christian prophet, works with the typical 'already-not-yet' perspective on eschatology held by all the New Testament writers. We do not yet see the final consummation of the kingdom of God we long for, but we dare to believe we have been shown something of that ultimate state of affairs; we dare to believe that the one creator God is in control of all things, and that Jesus Christ, the slain Lamb, has already won the decisive battle over Satan and evil in His cross and resurrection. His followers are therefore challenged to live faithful to him by refusing to compromise with the idolatrous culture of Empire, and by being willing to suffer loss and even death in order to participate in his triumph. A Beatitude (or 'blessing' – the first of seven) is attached to faithfully responding to the prophetic word when it is read aloud.

Revelation, then, challenges us with the question: Who are you listening to? Revelation was never meant as a fix for our morbid curiosity about the end-times or current affairs; it is a prophetic message intended to be heard and obeyed. It speaks with urgency as a timely message for its day.

A letter for churches

Thirdly, Revelation is not only an apocalypse and a prophecy, but is also a pastoral *letter* to the churches in John's care (Rev. 1:4). Like every other part of Scripture, John's revelation is concerned with what we see (an apocalypse) and what we hear (prophecy) because it is concerned with how we live and whom we worship.

All Christians are urged to listen, effectively being told:

Do not abandon your first love; be faithful even unto death; stay repent and eschew idolatry; hold fast to what you have been taught; wake up because you are dying out; hold firm, don't settle for anything less than the best God has to give; keep your love white hot; and always keep the door open to King Jesus – it's His Church, not ours.

John's first readers were situated in the context of the first-century Roman world. When John saw his first overwhelming vision of Jesus, he was told to write what he saw – and what he wrote was meant to be read aloud and received by those with ears to 'hear what the Spirit was saying to the churches' (Rev. 2:7).

This must govern our interpretation. With this in mind, we need to approach Revelation as we would other letters in the New Testament – with our priority being to interpret the text in context. Before we indulge in end-time speculation, we must make a serious effort to understand the book on its own terms as a message addressed to Christian in first century Asia Minor.

The letters in Revelation introduce the rest of prophecy and must be kept in mind all the way through it. Notice, for example, that 'he who conquers' (Rev. 2:7,11,17 etc) needs to be understood alongside what 'conquering' will mean; namely, a call to engage in the battle described in the central chapters, with a view to sharing in the glorious destiny depicted at the end of the book (Rev. 12:10).

The letters do address various local contexts and the specific issues of each of the seven churches, but all are warned, encouraged and consoled against the backdrop of the cosmic battle against evil for the kingdom of God.

Suffice to ask: Where would you need to be located to discover who really rules the world? Rome or Patmos?

John knows the answer because he is 'in the Spirit on the Lord's day'. In the Spirit he sees a throne, and on it the Sovereign Lord and the lamb who was slain.

Whatever else might be unclear, we do know that in the end God wins, that in Jesus the decisive battle has already been won, and that victory remains with love: 'Fear not, I am the first and the last, and the living one. I died, and behold I am alive for evermore' (Rev. 1:18).

Another thing worth considering is that John was writing as an exile on the island of Patmos, sharing with his churches the 'tribulation and the kingdom and the patient endurance' (Rev. 1:9). This mirrors the situation of John's original readers during the reign of the Emperor Domitian around AD 96. There is little evidence of persecution of Christians in Domitian's reign to a degree any worse than under previous emperors. But persecution and martyrdom (under Nero for example) was certainly a keen memory and John gives a clear warning of tougher times ahead in a coming day of trial.

Equally threatening for John's readers was the insidious and seductive pressure to conform to the idolatrous economic consumerism of the Roman Empire, sanctified by its religious system, which sought conformity and unswerving allegiance.

What, then, was the original purpose of Revelation?
- To encourage and warn the believers in Asia Minor against assimilation to the Roman Empire's values and systems.
- To exhort them to embrace suffering (and martyrdom, if necessary), as the price of faithfulness to Jesus. If the 'millennium' (mentioned once in Rev. 20:2) means anything at all, it probably, and symbolically, celebrates the triumph of the martyrs whose vindication is a theme tune of the book (Rev 20:4; 6:9–11).
- To assure them of the ultimate triumph of God the Lamb, both now and at the end of history.

Revelation is a book for *our time* because it motivates us, as it did John's hearers, to faithful living in the sure and certain hope of God's sovereignty and Christ's victory over evil. It is an urgent prophetic word of God to us in our day, a pastoral challenge to us to rediscover our distinctiveness as the Church through an unveiling of the real issues – the real battle going on behind the scenes of our routine daily lives and how we may overcome.

All about worship

Lastly, this prophetic apocalypse and pastoral letter is above all a Spirit-inspired vision of true worship.

John's pastoral vision sought to alert his readers to the fact that 'as kings and priests' (Rev. 1:6), they already share through worship in ruling the world. This flies in the face of the false news the Empire broadcasts and the growing cult of 'the Emperor as divine' it was promoting. There are, not surprisingly, seven scenes of worship in Revelation all located in 'heaven' (Rev. 4:2–11; 5:8–14; 7:9–17; 11:15–18; 14:1–5; 15:2-4; 19:1–8). These scenes act like the chorus in a Broadway musical or a Bach Passion, often explaining the vision that precedes.

By overhearing the worship of heaven, John's readers can be assured that 'the kingdom of the world has become the kingdom of our Lord and His Christ and he shall reign for ever and ever' (Rev. 11:15), and so be motivated to enter into worship on earth with greater passion and purpose. Throughout Revelation, these worship scenes re-emphasise that 'glory and power' belong to God, not the emperor; that the Lamb, not Caesar, is Lord.

Chapter 13 most graphically pictures the battle for worship that is raging. The three monsters – dragon, sea beast and land beast – form an 'unholy trinity', seeking to divert true worship from God to secular idols. John urges his readers to reject such blasphemous worship of the emperor at whatever cost (Rev. 13:10) and to worship God and the Lamb alone (Rev. 5:13–14).

A prophetic apocalypse and pastoral letter achieves its true goal when Christian readers are stirred to worship and are lost in wonder, love and praise. What all heaven declares, we declare. Revelation is resistance literature on many fronts. Perhaps only a suffering church fully understands its bracing message.

We have met the Alpha and Omega, the one who stands at the start and at the end of the story. And we have His word: 'I am coming soon'.

We start singing the doxology now, before the end.

'To him who loves us and has freed us from our sins by his blood and made us a kingdom, priests to his God and Father, to him be glory and dominion for ever and ever. Amen.' (Rev. 1:5–6)

Revelation motivates us to faithful living in the sure and certain hope of God's sovereignty and Christ's victory over evil.

*Eugene Peterson, *Reversed Thunder: The Revelation of John and the Praying Imagination* (New York: Harper & Row, 1988), p xi.

10
Now and not yet

It is worth knowing what accounts for the spiritual vibrancy of the New Testament.

More than sixty years ago, J.B. Phillips set out to translate the New Testament into Modern English. His aim was to do in his day what Eugene Peterson's *The Message* has done in ours.

Looking back on his experience of translating from the original Greek, Phillips said it was like trying to 'rewire an old house with the electric current still switched on'.*

What accounts for this extraordinary spiritual vitality that bubbles up through the text wherever we read it with open hearts? I would suggest two answers to that question. First was the conviction of the New Testament writers that they were living in the 'last days'. The first Christians realised that the 'last days' had dawned in Jesus Christ, who had enacted the future kingdom of God ahead of time. They held the classic Jewish-trained mind-set that envisaged two ages: 'the present evil age' (Gal. 1:4) and the 'age to come' (Heb. 6:5).

The first Christians came to see that Jesus had inaugurated God's future among them, and demonstrated it by His words and actions (see Matt. 12:28). But they also realised that there was much more to come, as Jesus urged them to pray: 'Your kingdom come'. They were taught to position themselves as living 'between the times' – and as followers of Jesus, so do we:

> 'Now these things happened to them as an example, but they were written down for our instruction, on whom the end of the ages has come.' (1 Cor. 10:11)

Christians live in the overlap of the two ages. Now, in the present age, we experience forgiveness of sins and the new life of the age to come, but we do not yet see all that God intends to disclose in the future when the kingdom is consummated.

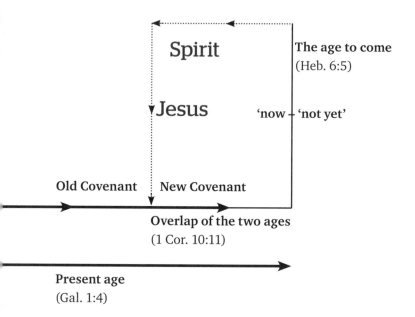

The 'now' and the 'not yet'

An important lesson to learn as Christians is to accept the dynamic tension of living realistically and hopefully in the 'now' and 'not yet':

> 'Now hope that is seen is not hope. For who hopes for what he sees? But if we hope for what we do not see, we wait for it with patience.' (Rom. 8:24–25)

Living in this dynamic tension requires wisdom. If we err too far on either side, we lose our balance and lose our place in the storyline. This happened with both the Galatians and the Corinthians, for opposite reasons.

Paul argued that the Galatians, under outside pressure, were in danger of relapsing into a spiritual time-warp, behaving as if they were in an earlier stage of the redemptive story and acting as if Christ had not come, by wanting to go back under the lordship of the Torah. The Corinthians, on the other hand, were getting ahead of themselves in the story, assuming they had arrived at the ultimate state of spiritual maturity when of course they had not. The Galatians were missing the 'now'; the Corinthians were forgetting the 'not yet'!

New Testament experience is a taste of the future now, of the 'powers of the age to come', of eternal life and final justification, a preview of the 'there and then' in the 'here and now'. No wonder the New Testament crackles with passion and resilience even amidst suffering!

In spirit and in truth

If we ask what accounts for the spiritual vitality behind the New Testament, the second answer is the empowering presence of the Holy Spirit which is a foretaste of future glory. But this must not be misconstrued as a content-less experience.

There seems to be a current trend in society for a vague, ill-defined 'spirituality': 'I am not religious but I am spiritual' is how many people see themselves. But for Christians, this is totally inadequate. For us, spirituality is Spirit-uality. And the Holy Spirit, mysterious as the wind as He is, is not ill-defined or undifferentiated. He is the Spirit of truth, poured out in the last days and intent on endorsing God's final self-revelation in Jesus Christ His Son (John 16:7–15).

Nowhere is this more keenly insisted on than in the first letter of John. John leads the way in quality-control, outlining several tests by which spiritual experience can be measured. Are Christians without sin? No, that's self-deception (1 John 1:8). Is it inevitable that we sin? No, that's cheap grace, but 'if' we sin, the remedy is close at hand (1 John 2:2; 3:6). Is our love genuine? Well, let's take the test:

'But if anyone has the world's goods and sees his brother in need, yet closes his heart against him, how does God's love abide in him? Little children, let us not love in word or talk but in deed and in truth.' (1 John 3:17–18)

How do we know that God is a God of love?

'In this the love of God was made manifest among us, that God sent his only Son into the world, so that we might live through him. In this is love, not that we have loved God but that he loved us and sent his Son to be the propitiation for our sins.' (1 John 4:9–10)

We cannot know God's love except as defined by the cross. That's the test.

The Holy Spirit is the Spirit of truth and will never contradict or detract from Jesus, but will glorify and promote Him. What we confess as the revealed truth about Jesus is the benchmark for testing spiritual experience:

'By this you know the Spirit of God: every spirit that confesses that Jesus Christ has come in the flesh is from God, and every spirit that does not confess Jesus is not from God.' (1 John 4:2–3)

In spirit and in truth then – is the secret to the vibrant life surging just beneath the surface of the text of the New Testament. And feeling this life flowing from God's future into us, we live joyfully in hope. I can't summarise this better than J.B. Phillips does in his translation of this passage from Romans:

> *'In my opinion whatever we may have to go through now is less than nothing compared with the magnificent future God has planned for us. The whole creation is on tiptoe to see the wonderful sight of the sons of God coming into their own. It is plain to anyone with eyes to see that at the present time all created life groans in a sort of universal travail. And it is plain, too, that we who have a foretaste of the Spirit are in a state of painful tension, while we wait for that redemption of our bodies which will mean that at last we have realised our full sonship in him. We were saved by this hope, but in our moments of impatience let us remember that hope always means waiting for something that we haven't yet got. But if we hope for something we cannot see, then we must settle down to wait for it in patience.'* (Rom. 8:18–25, J.B. Phillips)

This, for me, is the highest mountain peak of prophetic vision to found in the New Testament. The air is thinner here, more rarefied. We gaze achingly into God's good future. We gasp for breath with the wonder of what we glimpse. Then we descend as we must to the world as we know it, to find it groaning for its own deliverance, and we are dared to believe that its groans are the birth pangs of a better world coming. In solidarity with it, the Spirit groans too – and fills us with a measure of divine discontent. But we take heart that 'the sufferings of this present time are not worth comparing with the glory that is to be revealed to us'.

So we renew our pilgrimage with patience and prayer, fortified by a hope that passes understanding. For sure, absolute certainty is denied us. But we can share Paul's rock-solid confidence, and be convinced by the cross and empty tomb that...

Nothing will ever be able to separate us from the love of God in Christ Jesus our Lord.

*Cited by Lloyd Ogilvie in *Leadership Handbook of Preaching and Worship*, edited by James D. Berkley (Grand Rapids, MI, USA: Baker Publishing Group, 1997)

Further reading

On the New Testament:
G.K. Beale and D.A. Carson (Eds.), *Commentary on the New Testament use of the Old Testament* (Nottingham: Apollos, 2007)

William Lane, *Highlights of the Bible: The New Testament* (London: Regal, 1980)

On the covenantal structure and storyline of the Bible:
Philip Greenslade, *A Passion for God's Story* (Farnham: CWR, 2006)

Chris Wright, *Knowing Jesus Through the Old Testament: Rediscovering the roots of our faith* (Basingstoke: Marshall Pickering, 1992)

On the apostolic letters:
E. Randolph Richards, *Paul and First Century Letter Writing* (Downers Grove, IL, USA: IVP, 2004)

On the Gospels:
Richard Bauckham (Ed.), *The Gospels for all Christians: Rethinking the Gospel Audiences* (London: T&T Clark, 1998)

Richard B. Hays, *Reading Backwards* (London: SPCK, 2015)

Tom Wright, *How God Became King: The Forgotten Story of the Gospels* (San Francisco, USA: HarperOne, 2012)

On Acts and beyond:
Larry W. Hurtado, *Destroyer of the gods: Early Christian Distinctiveness in the Roman World* (Waco, TX, USA: Baylor University Press, 2016)

Ben Witherington III, *New Testament History: A Narrative Account* (Baker Academic & Paternoster Press, 2001)

On Hebrews:
Jonathan Griffiths (Ed.), *The Perfect Saviour: Key Themes in Hebrews* (Westmont, IL, USA: Inter-Varsity Press, 2012)

William. L. Lane, *Hebrews: A Call to Commitment* (Peabody, MA, USA: Hendrickson, 1985)

On Revelation:
Richard Bauckham, *The Theology of the Book of Revelation* (Cambridge: CUP, 1993)

Eugene Peterson, *Reversed Thunder: The Revelation of John and the Praying Imagination* (New York: Harper & Row, 1988)

Also available from Philip Greenslade

10 things worth knowing about
The Old Testament

This book will help you engage with the Scriptures that Jesus knew and loved. Understand passages in context and appreciate how and why they are God's Word for us today.

Drawing on his 40 years of biblical teaching experience, Philip illuminates ten key aspects from the Old Testament.

Available direct from CWR or from a Christian bookshop. Find out more about Philip Greenslade's books and courses at **www.cwr.org.uk**